THE BILL OF OBLIGATIONS

ALSO BY RICHARD HAASS

The World: A Brief Introduction

A World in Disarray

Foreign Policy Begins at Home

War of Necessity, War of Choice

The Opportunity

The Bureaucratic Entrepreneur

The Reluctant Sheriff

Intervention

Conflicts Unending

Beyond the INF Treaty

Congressional Power

EDITED VOLUMES

Honey and Vinegar

Transatlantic Tensions

Economic Sanctions and American Diplomacy

Superpower Arms Control

The BILL of OBLIGATIONS

——

THE TEN HABITS OF GOOD CITIZENS

——

RICHARD HAASS

PENGUIN PRESS   NEW YORK   2023

PENGUIN PRESS
An imprint of Penguin Random House LLC
penguinrandomhouse.com

LIBRARY OF CONGRESS CATALOGING-IN-PUBLICATION DATA
Names: Haass, Richard, author.
Title: The bill of obligations : the ten habits of good citizens / Richard Haass.
Description: New York : Penguin Press, [2023] | Includes index.
Identifiers: LCCN 2022028892 | ISBN 9780525560654 (hardcover) |
ISBN 9780525560661 (ebook)
Subjects: LCSH: Citizenship—United States. | Democracy—United States. |
Political culture—United States. | State, The.
Classification: LCC JF801 .H23 2023 | DDC 323.6—dc23/eng/20220922
LC record available at https://lccn.loc.gov/2022028892

Printed in the United States of America
1st Printing

Book design by Daniel Lagin

*To those Americans who put country and Constitution
before personal gain or party and stood up
for our democracy when it was most in danger*

CONTENTS

PREFACE

I have spent my career studying, practicing, writing about, and speaking on American foreign policy, and a question I frequently hear is "Richard, what keeps you up at night?" Often, even before I get to answer, the person posing the question suggests potential answers. Is it China? Russia? North Korea? Iran? Terrorism? Climate change? Cyberattacks? Another pandemic?

In recent years I started responding in a way that surprised me and many in the room. The most urgent and significant threat to American security and stability stems not from abroad but from within, from political divisions that for only the second time in U.S. history have raised questions about the future of American democracy and even the United States itself. These divisions also make it near impossible for the United States to address many of its economic, social, and political problems or to realize its potential. Many Americans (for a range of reasons) share my concern; according to a recent poll, a plurality (21 percent) believe that "threats to democracy" is the most important issue facing the country, surpassing cost of living, the economy, immigration, and climate change.

The deterioration of our democracy also has adverse consequences for our country's ability to contend with Russian aggression, a much more capable and assertive China, and a host of other regional and global challenges. Deep political divisions make it difficult—or even impossible—to design and implement a steady foreign policy at a time when what happens in the world deeply affects what happens at home. Similarly, a country at war with itself cannot set an example that people elsewhere will want to emulate. If democracy fails here, democracy will be endangered everywhere.

The storming of the U.S. Capitol on January 6, 2021, along with other attempts to overturn a free and fair election, made clear America's internal divisions had reached a qualitatively different and dangerous level. There is overwhelming evidence that members of Congress as well as the then president of the United States and his close associates were not only aware of what was being planned but were intimately involved. And even though Inauguration Day took place two weeks later, even though American democracy proved resilient, the outcome might have been different had it not been for the courage and character of a few state officials, Capitol police, and the serving vice president. It was a close-run thing—much too close for comfort.

What is more, the threat to American democracy is not limited to those who stormed the Capitol or the elected officials who cheered them on. An equally serious threat stems from the slow but steady erosion of popular support for democracy's underpinnings.

Before going on, I should perhaps say a few things about myself and what motivated me to write this book. I am not particularly partisan. I have worked for one Democratic senator, one Democratic president, and three Republican presidents. I began my political odyssey as a liberal Democrat, someone opposed to the war in Vietnam. My ideas began to change when I did my graduate work at Oxford in the 1970s, during which time I studied more history, read Aleksandr Solzhenitsyn's powerful denunciations of the Soviet system, and watched up close the illiberalism of the British Labour Party and the rise of a principled Margaret Thatcher. For most of my adult life I was a registered Republican, although in the summer of 2020 I reluctantly concluded I was no longer comfortable in that party and changed to no party affiliation. But even when I was a Republican I would at times vote for Democrats. Party was never as important to me as individual candidates and issues. As I write this, I serve as the president of the Council on Foreign Relations, an institution dedicated to being a nonpartisan resource for Americans across the political spectrum on questions of U.S. foreign policy and the country's relationship with the world.

In short, what led to this book is not my political preferences.

I am motivated by what keeps me up at night: our democracy is imperiled, and its demise would be an incalculable loss to this country's citizens and to the world. My belief is that it can be saved only if Americans across the political spectrum come to accept that citizenship involves more than their asserting—or the government's protecting—what they understand to be their rights.

I have come around to the view that our very concept of citizenship needs to be revised, or better yet expanded, if American democracy is to survive. As two leading political scientists wrote in a classic study, "The development of a stable and effective democratic government depends upon more than the structures of government and politics: it depends upon the orientations that people have to the political process—upon the political culture." Yes, respect for individual rights remains basic to the functioning of this or any democracy, but rights alone do not a successful democracy make. A democracy that concerns itself only with protecting and advancing individual rights will find itself in jeopardy, as rights will come into conflict with one another. When they inevitably do, it is essential that there is a path for citizens to compromise or a willingness to coexist peacefully and work with those with whom they disagree.

Beyond rights, obligations are the other cornerstone of a successful democracy—obligations between individual citizens as well as between citizens and their government. Obligations—akin to what Danielle Allen calls "habits of citizenship"—are things that should happen but that the law cannot require. Without a culture of obligation coexisting alongside a commitment to rights, American democracy could well come undone. We need nothing less than a "Bill of Obligations" to guide how we teach, understand, and conduct our politics.

I write in full awareness that I have long been associated with the establishment—people and institutions that have often been vilified and blamed for the failures of democracy. Some of these criticisms are well-founded. The purpose of this book is not to defend the past. It is to help build our common future, to remind readers why democracy should be cherished and suggest what could be done to preserve it. What fills these pages is a mixture of reflection and advocacy, written out of aspiration.

Implicit in all this is the conviction that American democracy is most decidedly worth keeping. The American experiment has with one obvious exception managed to sort out its differences without experiencing civil conflict on a large scale. This worthy experiment has been a sanctuary for tens of millions of immigrants fleeing persecution or seeking opportunity, and a safe harbor for political expression and religious freedom. Our nation is also an engine of innovation, creating unprecedented wealth for hundreds of millions of people and increasing average life expectancy by decades for its citizens. Beyond its borders, the United States proved central to defeating fascism in World War II, navigating a Cold War that ended peacefully and on terms largely consistent with American interests and values, and fashioning a world order that for all its flaws ended the colonial era and built international arrangements that have brought greater prosperity, freedom, and health to literally billions of people.

Yet American democracy has also come up short in meaningful ways. There is an enormous gap between the words of the Declaration of Independence—"that all men are created equal, that they are endowed by their creator with certain unalienable rights, that among these are life, liberty, and the pursuit of happiness"— and reality, including but not limited to the treatment of Native Americans and the institution of slavery and the status of women. This country has failed to adequately deal with discrimination based on race, gender, religion, or country of origin. Equal opportunity for many has been a hope rather than a reality. Nor has the country always lived up to its stated values and principles abroad, frequently supporting leaders who showed little fidelity to democratic values or the rule of law.

But progress—slow and winding—has been made over the decades toward America fulfilling its promise. The hard-fought passage of the Thirteenth through Fifteenth, as well as the Nineteenth, Amendments to the Constitution, civil rights legislation, the legalization of same-sex marriage—all demonstrate that this country has an ability to recognize and correct mistakes and introduce political reform and policy change. This is another built-in advantage of democracies. Certainly more must be done, but as Winston Churchill put it, "No one pretends that democracy is perfect or all-wise. Indeed it has been said that democracy is the worst form of government except for all those other forms that have been tried."

The stakes for the United States and its approximately 330 million citizens are difficult to exaggerate. Inability to come to agreement on policies to strengthen American democracy has the potential to disrupt the economy and society alike. Essential public services could deteriorate or break down entirely. Political rights taken for granted could be suspended or compromised. Violence on a large scale, be it by ordinary criminals or those with a political agenda, the latter meeting the definition of terrorism, has become all too imaginable. And although an overwhelming majority of Americans oppose it, attempted secession from the union by one or more states cannot be dismissed out of hand.

Moreover, what is at stake does not end at the water's edge, at the country's borders. A United States that is divided and defined by politics will be in no condition to set an example that others will want to emulate. This was a theme central to President Jimmy Carter's inaugural address: "Our nation can be strong abroad only if it is strong at home. And we know that the best way to enhance freedom in other lands is to demonstrate here that our democratic system is worthy of emulation." The perceived failure of American democracy to function and deliver provides an opportunity for authoritarian regimes to justify their repression of their own citizens and others. In order to deter would-be foes and provide security to friends and allies, Americans must be able to come together across partisan divides. Our current political atmosphere is a recipe for diminished U.S. influence, the expansion of Chinese and Russian sway, the proliferation of nuclear weapons, and increased conflict in the world. As I argued in a book published nearly a decade ago, foreign policy begins at home.

After January 6, Chinese television was filled with images of the violence and disarray at the Capitol. This is instructive. China and its government-dominated authoritarian model would likely be the principal beneficiaries if democracy here were to fail. Those who purport to be tough on China are being anything but if they weaken democracy here in the United States. Similarly, a country paralyzed by internal divisions will be in no condition to help shape international responses to global challenges that could define this century, including but not limited to infectious disease, climate change, the spread of nuclear weapons, and terrorism. All of this would come at great cost to Americans and to others, as little stays local for long in a globalized world.

The question is whether we the people will meet these challenges. My goal is to see that we do. My assessment is that doing so is essential, as democracy cannot otherwise be preserved. Part One of this book begins with a discussion of how rights came to occupy so central a place in American democracy and goes on to examine the mounting evidence that this rights-based democracy is failing. Part Two of the book sets out ten obligations that, if adopted by a preponderance of citizens, would go a long way toward fixing American democracy. Putting these obligations into practice, however, is up to us.

PART ONE

——

The Crisis of Our Rights-Based Democracy

——

Rights and Their Limits

Democracy (literally "rule of the people") gives the citizens of a country decisive power. In principle, such power could be exercised directly. Several democracies at the national and state level maintain options for the people to decide matters of policy. California often has turned to referenda to decide important issues. Similarly, the United Kingdom's decision to leave the European Union (Brexit) was decided by popular referendum. The problem with direct democracy is that most citizens lack the time, interest, or expertise to run their societies. There is also the danger (pointed out by the founders of America's political system) that direct or self-rule could easily degenerate into a tyranny of the majority at the expense of minorities. And there is the reality that complex, consequential issues do not lend themselves to being decided by popular vote, as outcomes can be heavily influenced by misleading public statements and the immediate political context.

The response to such concerns with direct democracy was and is republicanism—not in the sense of the party by that name, but rather representative governments exercising authority in the name of the people and held accountable to them. It is one thing to set out to do this in principle, however, and quite another to succeed in practice. This was the experience of the United States of America in its first decade. The Constitution's preamble includes this memorable phrase: "in order to form a more perfect union." The union already existed before the Constitution was adopted in 1788, twelve years after the country declared its independence from Great Britain.

The Constitution was in fact the second attempt to provide a blueprint for the federal government and its relationship with the states and citizens—Constitution 2.0 in modern parlance. The first attempt, the Articles of Confederation, had entered into force in March 1781. The critical word here is "confederation." A confederation is made up of sovereign elements that come together for limited purposes and in a manner that does not encroach upon the independent status of the component parts. All of which is to say that the Articles of Confederation were almost exclusively about the prerogatives of the thirteen founding states. The second article makes this explicit: "Each state retains its sovereignty, freedom, and independence, and every power, jurisdiction, and right, which is not by this confederation expressly delegated to the United States." Hardly any power, jurisdiction, or significant role was assigned to the national (federal) government. The political union was described as a "firm league of friendship" even though there was nothing firm and little that was friendly about it. Not surprisingly, frustration with the Articles mounted during and after the successful Revolutionary War. The new country found itself broke and unable to defend itself. Delegates from twelve of the thirteen states (Rhode Island opted out) convened in Philadelphia in May 1787 to amend the Articles. Before long the vast majority concluded that the Articles were so flawed that amending them would not be sufficient. Instead, they sought a fresh start and began working on a new document providing for how the country was to be governed.

It was one thing for there to be agreement that the Articles were inadequate, quite something else for the delegates to agree on what should take their place. A number of fault lines quickly emerged. There were splits between delegates from populous states, who favored political power distributed in a manner proportionate to the number of people, and those from states with fewer people, who wanted each state to have the same say, regardless of population or size. There were ideological differences between those who supported a more democratic system (in which power would reside mostly in bodies reflecting popular preferences or at least the preferences of those permitted to vote) and those advocating for a system in which those wielding power would be appointed. Yet a third axis of difference and debate was over the relationship between the states and the central government and above all the balance of power between them. Hovering in the background was the issue of slavery; while still present in twelve of the thirteen original states, it was central to some and fading in others, and there was already a question of whether the federal government would limit slavery in territories or states seeking to join the union. Indeed, James Madison concluded that the greatest divide was not between states with large and small populations but between North and South.

There was, however, considerable agreement among the delegates that there needed to be a clear allocation of power and authority to the government, but that this power and authority needed to be distributed carefully. This idea of checks and balances was central to the pro-Constitution arguments of James Madison, Alexander Hamilton, and John Jay, the three authors of *The Federalist Papers*, arguably the most important and influential documents relating to American democracy other than the Constitution. In Madison's view, the interior structure of the government had to be such that "its several constituent parts may, by their mutual relations, be the means of keeping each other in their proper places. . . . Ambition must be made to counteract ambition."

Toward this end, power was divided among or shared by the legislative, executive, and judicial branches of the new national government. The details were spelled out in the first three articles of the new Constitution. The animating idea was to limit any concentration of power. The legislature and the courts were also given the ability to investigate and, if need be, remove public officials from office through the mechanism of impeachment and trial.

The more relevant component of checks and balances, though, came through a structure of shared or overlapping powers. Legislation that authorizes major initiatives and provides funding for them must be passed into law by a majority of both chambers of Congress and then signed into law by the president. If the president rejects the legislation—this is what is meant by using the veto power—the legislation dies unless two-thirds of both the House of Representatives and the Senate vote to override the veto. Nominations to cabinet-level positions as well as a good many other influential posts require Senate confirmation, i.e., approval by a majority. The same holds for appointments to the Supreme Court and many other judicial positions. Congress must authorize and appropriate funds for any and all purposes, from national security (including defense, diplomacy, and foreign aid) to all things domestic. Certain specific powers in the realm of foreign policy and national security are also shared. The Senate must approve nominations for individuals to serve as ambassador. Treaties with foreign countries must be approved by two-thirds of the Senate. Congress is given the power to declare war, but here, as elsewhere, a good deal of unilateral authority to make decisions and carry them out has moved to the executive branch and the president.

Little was explicit when it came to the judiciary in the Constitution; it is not just that it is given short shrift, with Article III requiring just six paragraphs, but its powers are not specified. It is not surprising then that Alexander Hamilton describes the judiciary as incontestably the weakest of the three branches of government, saying it "will always be the least dangerous to the political rights of the Constitution." Unlike the legislature or the executive, the judiciary according to Hamilton "has no influence over the sword or the purse" and possesses "neither force nor will but merely judgment." Less than two decades later, though, in 1803, the Supreme Court (in deciding the landmark case of *Marbury v. Madison*) established the ability of the courts to rule on whether a law or action of either the legislative branch or the executive or any state is consistent with the Constitution. What has expanded over the centuries is the notion of judicial review, with an increasingly powerful Court frequently deciding on differences stemming from competing interpretations of the Constitution.

The delegates to the Constitutional Convention were preoccupied with the question of what was to be the authority and role of the national government. The Articles may have been unworkable, but many feared that what would replace them would create a government and above all an executive too strong. Patrick Henry, the Virginian best known for his fiery declaration "Give me liberty or give me death," exemplified this stance. "This Constitution is said to have beautiful features; but when I come to examine these features, sir, they appear to me horribly frightful. Among other deformities, it has an awful squinting; it squints towards monarchy; and does not this raise indignation in the breast of every true American? Your President may easily become king. . . . Where are your checks in this government? Your strongholds will be in the hands of your enemies." Compromise was central to resolving this debate. The essence of the compromise was to explicitly limit the role of the new federal government, and the executive in particular, so that states and citizens maintained substantial independence. The principal mechanism for accomplishing this—and assuring the approval of the new Constitution itself—was through the adoption of the Bill of Rights, ten specific amendments to the Constitution that constrained the newly reformed federal government. In 1791, the Bill of Rights became the law of the land.

As is the case with the Ten Commandments, the first ten amendments to the Constitution are a mixture of the negative and the positive, what is not to be done and what is called for. The First Amendment protects the exercise of religion and prohibits establishing an official state religion along the lines of the Church of England in the United Kingdom. It guarantees both freedom *of* religion and freedom *from* religion. The First Amendment also provides for the freedoms of speech (for political purposes), the press, assembly, and petition of government for any grievances. The Second Amendment addresses the right of the people to keep and bear arms. The Third Amendment limits unwanted quartering of soldiers in homes; the Fourth protects citizens against unreasonable searches and seizures.

The Fifth through Eighth Amendments deal with legal issues and among other things prohibit double jeopardy (being tried twice for the same alleged crime) and being required to provide testimony against oneself (hence the ability to "plead the Fifth"), and they guarantee due process, including a speedy and public trial by an impartial jury that also includes counsel for the defense and the right to call and hear witnesses. These amendments also rule out excessive bail, cruel and unusual punishment, and the ability of the government to seize property for public use without paying the owner proper compensation.

The Ninth Amendment is a catchall, making clear that the enumeration of certain rights does not mean others are not retained by the people, as is the Tenth Amendment, which reserves powers not explicitly granted by the Constitution to the states or individuals.

These initial amendments were adopted to prevent the newly strengthened national government from acquiring too much power. The chosen remedy was to explicitly enumerate and protect the rights of states and individuals. The biggest shortcoming of the Bill of Rights was its failure to address the most serious flaws of the Constitution, above all by declining to extend rights to enslaved people, women, Indigenous peoples, and the poor. The first ten amendments did nothing to counteract the so-called three-fifths compromise, by which an enslaved person was counted as three-fifths of a free person for the purpose of determining the number of citizens in a state. Nor did they eliminate or shorten the period (twenty years) during which enslaved persons could be brought ("imported") into the country. The Bill of Rights also failed to counter the constitutional provision that fugitive slaves be returned to their owners. Put differently, the Bill of Rights made progress in protecting individuals against the federal government but not the states.

Only with the adoption of several additional amendments to the Constitution (above all, the Thirteenth and Fourteenth Amendments) in the aftermath of the Civil War were slavery and involuntary servitude banned and citizenship, with its rights and privileges, extended; as Michael Sandel has written, "The Civil War resolved what the Constitution had not, and established the supremacy of the national government over the states." The Fourteenth Amendment further reinforced the primacy of the federal government vis-à-vis states (something already expressed in Article VI of the Constitution) and strengthened the hands of individuals vis-à-vis states, underscoring that "no State shall make or enforce any law which shall abridge the privileges or immunities of citizens of the United States; nor shall any State deprive any person of life, liberty, or property without due process of law nor deny to any person within its jurisdiction the equal protection of the laws." The Fifteenth Amendment (adopted approximately 150 years ago) specifically extended the right to vote to all men regardless of race or color; the Nineteenth Amendment (adopted a century ago) did the same for women. The Twenty-sixth Amendment (adopted half a century ago) barred any state or locality from preventing anyone who had reached the age of eighteen from voting.

With these amendments and the passage of time, a political system has emerged that is meant to limit the role and reach of government and allow individuals the freedom to speak, publish, and broadcast what they please, to advocate and organize for what they seek, to practice (or not practice) religion as they see fit, to start a business and accumulate wealth, to keep and bear arms, and a good deal else. Just as important as the law is the existence of institutions and procedures that can be used if and when the law is violated and treatment is unequal.

Nevertheless, the struggle over rights, what Abraham Lincoln described in November 1863 at Gettysburg as the nation's "unfinished work," continues to this day. A rights-based approach to citizenship is pervasive and is common to those on the political left and right alike; what distinguishes them is which rights they emphasize and support and which they oppose. Abortion, just to choose one example, is an issue in which those who oppose the practice talk about defending the rights of the unborn, while those who support it emphasize the right of the mother to choose. Then there is the question of what limits should be set on what can be said or written on social media and who should set those limits. There is of course the long-standing debate over which guns and ammunition should be proscribed and who should have access to what is allowed and under what conditions. Today there are pitched battles over state laws that in one way or another place obstacles on the ease of voting. Those on the political right argue such limits are needed to guarantee the integrity of the electoral process; those on the left see such laws as vehicles to disenfranchise minorities and other citizens living in areas known to vote Democratic. There is the growing debate over parental rights when it comes to determining what children are taught in schools. And there are deeply held differences amid the COVID-19 pandemic over whether the government can insist that individuals should wear face masks and get vaccinated or if they should have the right to decide for themselves.

Another recurring debate in this country concerns what the government owes every citizen beyond basic safety. It is akin to what Franklin Delano Roosevelt called "freedom from want." The Great Depression in the 1930s changed the conversation on this, and it has evolved since then, ratcheting up in intensity amid the reforms of President Lyndon B. Johnson's Great Society in the 1960s, and, more recently, in the aftermath of the 2007–2008 financial crisis and the COVID-19 pandemic. At issue is what ought to constitute the minimum safety net for every citizen. The debate thus encompasses what should be provided by the government— be it federal, state, or local—and involves such issues as minimum wage levels, access to health care, retirement income, support for children, paid leave, accommodations for those with disabilities, unemployment insurance, and guaranteed income levels regardless of whether the individual is willing and able to work. A related debate is how such government standards and programs should be funded.

This book will not join these debates. My point in mentioning them reflects the reality that many of our most intractable and vicious political battles emerge when we have conflicting beliefs about the rights to which people are entitled. Yes, discussions over what political rights should be protected and what economic rights should be extended are critical, but these issues are already being intensely studied and debated. Instead, the aim here is to focus on another, often overlooked dimension of citizenship. I am speaking here of obligations, of what citizens owe one another and the country.

Obligations are different from requirements. Americans are required to observe the law, pay taxes, serve on juries, and respond to a military draft if there is one. There is no wiggle room. Failure to meet requirements can result in a penalty, be it a fine, imprisonment, or both. Obligations are different, involving not what citizens must do but what they should do. They are defined here as moral and political rather than legal commitments to be undertaken voluntarily. They are intended to be greater than responsibilities, which are all too easily shirked. What makes obligations so important is that the ability of American democracy to endure and deliver what it can and should to its citizens depends on their being put into practice.

Placing obligations at the core of citizenship is necessary because the protection and promotion of political and economic rights inevitably lead to disagreements. As Supreme Court Justice Stephen Breyer pointed out, "Many of our cases, the most difficult cases, are not about right versus wrong. They are about right versus right." Any conversation about rights can quickly descend into one of competing absolutes. Some would describe the rights of the unborn as absolute, others the rights of the mother. Some believe any constraints on access to guns and munitions are unacceptable, others see such limits as essential for their right to be safe. Similar arguments have been put forward when it comes to mandates for masks and vaccines, with some maintaining any mandate infringes on free choice, others that mandates are needed for public health. There are intense debates over whether free speech is sacrosanct or if it requires limits when it includes assertions that are untrue and could cause damage to the safety of others or the fabric of democracy.

The ruler in an authoritarian system settles such disagreements by decree. In a democracy, differences must be resolved by a process judged to be fair and accepted as legitimate regardless of the ultimate decision. The question thus arises as to whether and how disagreements over rights or policies meant to protect specific rights are to be bridged and mediated. Rules are needed to prevent disagreements from hampering a necessary outcome or, worse yet, spilling over into violence. Supreme Court Justice Louis Brandeis once described "sunlight" as "the best of disinfectants" in a democracy; openness and transparency are better than anything else at rooting out corruption and the improper use of power. As gas is to an engine, think of obligations as the best fuel for a democracy, increasing the odds that it functions in a manner that serves its citizens well.

This is needed now more than ever because American democracy has come to focus almost exclusively on perceived rights and is breaking down as a result. The correct response is not to ignore rights or to stop trying to make this a more perfect union; to the contrary, this is unfinished work that demands attention. But this work needs to be carried out in a manner that strengthens democracy. This goes beyond the centuries-old debate over the "social contract," the understanding between the government and the governed in which the latter accept certain limits on their liberties in exchange for social order and above all a fundamental level of physical security. Here I can do no better than to quote the mid-twentieth century educator Max Arzt: "It is not enough to talk about human rights without emphasizing human duties.... Rights without duties lead to lawlessness, even as duties without rights can lead to slavery and to the abasement of individuality."

Democratic Deterioration

All of us should be worried about the future of the United States. Too many people fall back on the comfortable view that the American people have encountered difficult challenges in the past and have always come through. Winston Churchill, arguably the figure of greatest historic consequence in the previous century, is said to have remarked that "You can always count on Americans to do the right thing—after they've tried everything else." But is that true? Have things changed? And will what got us through the dark times in the past still work for us now?

When I began contemplating this book, we were two months into the eleven-week transition between the forty-fifth and forty-sixth presidents of the United States. It was already clear that something unprecedented was going on. The "peaceful transition of power" between the outgoing occupant of the Oval Office and his successor, which Americans had come to take for granted, was neither peaceful nor certain.

It is difficult to exaggerate how much this last sentence continues to surprise. The peaceful transition of power, its essence captured in the traditional limousine ride down Pennsylvania Avenue from the White House to Capitol Hill in which the soon-to-be former and the soon-to-be president share the back seat, is one of the hallmarks of American democracy. Candidates compete, voters vote, results are tabulated and announced, winners win and go on to govern, and losers concede and assume the mantle of loyal opposition.

In authoritarian countries such as China and Russia, no such process occurs. Legal limits as to how long a ruler can stay in power have been extended or jettisoned. In their stead is the prospect that the current ruler will rule until he does not. At that point, to be arrived at either when leaders are pushed out or no longer physically able to function, there will likely be a scramble for power. Large-scale violence and some version of martial law could well materialize. What is missing in these situations is a widely shared belief that the political process is legitimate, a belief that requires the process to be seen as fair and honest and representative. As a result, no one can predict with any confidence when or how Xi Jinping or Vladimir Putin will leave office, how disruptive the transition will be, or who or what will follow them.

Until recently, it was safe to assume this could not happen in the United States, that this country was, is, and always would be fundamentally different. After all, there have been more than forty transitions from one president to another, all without a hitch. Our transitions were peaceful even in times of war or after elections that were fiercely fought, in years where the loser believed the results were unfair and there was no love lost between the candidates. But this has now changed, as ever since November 2020 the forty-fifth president and many in his party have insisted despite an absence of supporting evidence that the results of a free and fair election were fraudulent and acted to overturn them. We—Americans—are not as exceptional as we like to think. The United States, the world's oldest democracy, is not immune to democratic backsliding, a trend worldwide over the past two decades. What we don't yet know is whether what happened in late 2020 and early 2021 was an aberration or a precedent. The fact that as of this writing a significant percentage of the population refuses to accept the results of the November 2020 election, and a meaningful number of those with leadership roles in the Republican Party are encouraging them not to, is evidence that something is seriously amiss.

I am well aware that there are those who disagree with me on this, believing that I am guilty of exaggerating. I participated in exchanges with two separate groups of people I both like and respect, one via email and another across a dinner table, in which it was argued that the events of 1968 presented a far more serious challenge to American democracy. For those too young (or old) to remember, that was a year defined by large-scale and at times violent protests against the Vietnam War, the assassinations of both the civil rights leader Martin Luther King Jr. and senator and presidential candidate Robert Kennedy, and urban riots. It was a terrible year. Still, order was restored, the assassinations were violent but not revolutionary acts, U.S. involvement in the Vietnam War began to wind down as the political leadership responded to a loss of public support, and the 1968 presidential election was carried out in an orderly fashion with its results widely accepted by both those who favored the outcome and those who did not.

Some of what is going on today can fairly be described as familiar. Politics have never been absent from policy making. George Washington warned about the dangers of what he called "faction" in his farewell address, delivered as he was stepping down from the presidency after two terms in office. The authors of *The Federalist Papers* similarly worried about how factions could threaten the functioning or even fabric of the country. Their definition of faction—"a number of citizens, whether amounting to a majority or minority of the whole, who are united and actuated by some common impulse of passion, or of interest, adverse to the rights of other citizens, or to the permanent and aggregate interests of the community"—is as relevant today as when it was originally written.

The question is whether things have not just continued as usual but gotten worse. What I have in mind here is our increasingly partisan, dysfunctional politics. Hundreds of senior-level jobs in the federal government go unfilled for extended periods as a small number of senators prevent nominations from being acted on for reasons unrelated to the person's qualifications. Many in Congress balk at voting to raise the federal debt ceiling even though a failure to increase the government's ability to raise more debt would cause financial havoc. The fact that the same members of Congress voted for the legislation that added to the government spending without approving taxes to cover it seems not to matter. Congressional leadership could not even agree to establish a bipartisan commission (along the lines of the commission formed to investigate the September 11, 2001, terrorist attacks) to investigate the events of January 6, 2021. Fewer bills become law than ever before; increasingly, legislation is either blocked or, using the so-called reconciliation process, passed by one party in a manner that allows it to work around the need to get a supermajority of sixty votes required to end a filibuster.

As worrisome as all this is, it is not as dangerous as other trends that set the stage for political crisis and widespread violence. January 6 involved not just violence by a few but by hundreds, violence supported or at least tolerated by the leadership and many elected representatives of the Republican Party in an effort to stop the counting and certification of electoral votes. Plans were developed to call on the military to impound voting machines absent any evidence they had been tampered with. The results of an election that was overwhelmingly free and fair have been rejected by tens of millions of Americans even though literally dozens of audits have shown the vote counts to be accurate. In Georgia, a law was passed that hands the state legislature enormous say over who would cast the state's electoral votes in future presidential elections. A number of other states are considering similar legislation. It is not difficult to imagine dueling sets of electors claiming to represent a state after a future presidential election, something that could well lead to the election of a president viewed as illegitimate by a significant number or even a majority of voters. Against such a backdrop the potential for widespread violence would increase sharply.

Violence need not come in the form of a second civil war, as some have suggested is possible. Such a relatively centralized, organized, two-sided, and traditional conflict, with a clear beginning and an end, is not likely to be America's future. But substantial politically inspired violence could well be. It would likely come in the form of acts of violence by and among armed, decentralized networks linked by social media. It could be triggered by a contested election, a controversial legal decision, or a protest that got out of hand. Targets could range from government buildings and officials to banks, stores, and even bars and restaurants known to be frequented by a particular group. The participants' agendas could be many and varied. Once begun, it would be difficult to contain given a lack of centralized leadership within such groups. If there is a model for what we should fear, it comes from Northern Ireland and the Troubles, the three-decade struggle starting in the late 1960s that involved multiple paramilitary groups, police, and soldiers and resulted in some 3,600 deaths and a sharp reduction in local economic output.

When I think of this terrible prospect I am reminded of an anecdote more than two centuries old. On what was to be the final day of the Constitutional Convention of 1787, a woman reportedly asked Benjamin Franklin, whom she encountered as he was walking away from Philadelphia's Independence Hall, what the delegates had decided. "A republic," replied Franklin. He then went on to add, somewhat ominously, "If you can keep it."

There is some debate as to whether this encounter ever happened. What is certain is that three-quarters of a century later, the answer to Franklin's question came close to being answered in the negative. Secession and civil war temporarily ruptured and nearly destroyed the United States of America. In the end, the country survived, although more than 600,000 Americans—a number roughly equivalent to between six and seven million as a percentage of today's population—did not. A century and a half since that initial test, the country's future is again in doubt. The question must thus again be asked about the republic: Can an increasingly divided American people keep it?

Doubts have long existed. None other than John Adams, the second president of the United States and the father of the sixth, wrote that "Democracy never lasts long. It soon wastes exhausts and murders itself. There never was a Democracy yet, that did not commit suicide." Or, as Abraham Lincoln said, "If destruction be our lot, we must ourselves be its author and finisher." History is replete with examples of democracies that died. One path comes from democracies being overthrown by their own militaries in sudden and sometimes violent coups d'état. This was a frequent occurrence during the four decades of the Cold War; examples include Greece, Pakistan, Chile, Argentina, Brazil, Ghana, Nigeria, and Turkey. And more recently we have seen such takeovers in Egypt, Thailand, and Myanmar (Burma).

The most worrisome and relevant historical pattern for American democracy, though, is that of democracies that decayed from within, sowing the seeds of their own demise. This was the fate of Weimar Germany in the 1930s at the hands of Adolf Hitler. More recently it describes what took place in Venezuela, first under Hugo Chávez and subsequently under Nicolás Maduro. Democratic deterioration on a large scale has also taken place in recent years in Russia, Turkey, Hungary, Poland, the Philippines, and a good many other countries. As Steven Levitsky and Daniel Ziblatt observed in *How Democracies Die*, "Since the end of the Cold War, most democratic breakdowns have been caused not by generals and soldiers but by elected governments themselves." There are always would-be demagogues and authoritarian figures in and around politics; what seems to matter most is the vulnerability of a political system to inviting them in and being hijacked by them.

Why is this happening now in the United States? To begin with, there has been a loss of common identity or nationhood. A country is both a political and legal entity. A nation is something different, representing a group of people with a common identity. The two terms are often conflated, assumed to be synonyms, when they are anything but. The loss of a common identity, the end to a single nation, can threaten the functioning or even survival of the country. It is increasingly hard to speak of a shared American experience, outlook, values, or priorities. Instead, the country is sharply divided, with a growing number of states either solidly "red" (invariably Republican or conservative leaning) or "blue" (consistently progressive or Democratic leaning). The number of purple or swing states is declining, along with the political center. It is difficult not to conjure William Butler Yeats, who observed, "Things fall apart; the centre cannot hold."

The United States has been around for close to two and a half centuries, but entities that were far older no longer exist, the consequence of the loss of a commitment to the whole that took precedence over the particular. Little is either inevitable or permanent; as former president Bill Clinton recently noted, "Freedom and democracy and the rule of law are not permanently enshrined just because we've survived two-hundred-plus years now." What makes the United States especially vulnerable to division is that the American nation, unlike that of many countries, is not based on ethnicity, race, heritage, language, or religion. The United States, which originally derived mostly from those with a European background—Native Americans were already here and enslaved persons were brought here involuntarily from Africa and the Caribbean—is truly diverse given subsequent waves of immigration from all over the world. The contrast with many mostly homogenous (in demographic terms) democracies in Asia (such as Japan and South Korea), Europe, and parts of Latin America is pronounced.

Adding to the challenge is that democracy is difficult. Democracy asks a great deal of its citizens and leaders alike. From the former it requires informed participation. From the latter it asks for good faith and restraint, and a willingness to put the collective interest before politics, party, or personal gain.

Before looking closely at the United States, it should be added that "democratic difficulty" or "democratic deterioration" is hardly limited to the world's oldest democracy. We see it in much of Latin America, where democratic reforms are in peril as populist leaders who have little patience with independent institutions take power. We also see it in parts of Europe, where center-left and center-right parties are losing ground to parties at both ends of the political spectrum—especially to what is best described as the illiberal right. There have been sudden coups in countries like Myanmar and slow-motion coups elsewhere. Meanwhile, hopes that more authoritarian countries would become more open have not materialized; to the contrary, the trend in the world over the past two decades is that authoritarian systems, including those of China, Russia, Iran, and North Korea, have become even more repressive.

There are some challenges, however, that are uniquely American. It is difficult to reform the American system; apart from the ten amendments that constitute the Bill of Rights, there have been only seventeen amendments to the Constitution since its adoption and none for the past thirty years. Under Article V of the Constitution, an amendment requires a two-thirds majority vote by both the Senate and the House of Representatives and then must be approved by a majority vote of three-fourths of the states. The procedural requirements are daunting. There is in principle an alternative path for considering amendments to the Constitution—a new constitutional convention, convened by a majority vote by two-thirds (thirty-four of fifty) of state legislatures—but this too is a high bar and has yet to happen in practice.

Moreover, the American system was designed for a population of just over three million, approximately 1 percent of the current total of more than 330 million. It was also built for a country of thirteen states concentrated on the eastern seaboard of the North American continent. Today's United States numbers fifty states and spans a three-thousand-mile-wide continent and well beyond. It cannot be taken for granted that a system of government can evolve sufficiently to take into account changes of this scale. In this case, it has not; if anything, the American political process has grown more sclerotic and more resistant to making things happen. There are literally tens of thousands of participants motivated by special interests of one sort or another, be they person, party, policy, or profit; by contrast, there are few such actors that can be said to be motivated by the national interest.

All of this is further exacerbated by the widening gap between populations and how they are represented in government. All states have two senators, which means that Wyoming, with a population of under six hundred thousand, has the same representation in the Senate as California, with a population of some forty million. Or think about it this way: twenty-two states with a combined population that approximates California's have forty-four of the seats in the Senate. The Founders believed that such a system would help prevent a tyranny of the majority, but in fact the country has ended up with something closer to a tyranny of the minority: while most Americans support gun control measures and a woman's right to choose, a minority has ensured there are few limits on the former and in some states have curtailed access to abortions. Today, a small number of states with a small percentage of the total population have an outsized influence on presidential elections, and as a result there is a growing gap between the popular vote and electoral outcomes. Both George W. Bush and Donald Trump lost the popular vote, in the latter's case by nearly three million votes, but were still elected president. Given the realities of the electoral college, candidates all but ignore states where they are sure to win or lose and concentrate their efforts on the handful of states that could tip the balance.

While there is no single development or event or person that explains matters, another force adding to the erosion of democracy is the fading of the belief that we are all part of the same community. One factor is economic inequality. Measures show that inequality is large and growing. George Packer, in his important book *Last Best Hope*, argues that "inequality destroys the sense of shared citizenship and with it self-government" and, similarly, that "at the heart of our divisions is almost half a century of rising inequality and declining social mobility."

I would argue, though, that even more important than the reality of economic inequality is the inequality of economic opportunity. Americans have lived with extreme examples of wealth since the country's inception. The nineteenth century had the Rockefellers, Carnegies, and Vanderbilts, in some ways all forerunners of Bill Gates, Jeff Bezos, Elon Musk, and Warren Buffett. What made it tolerable for the majority was the belief that real advances and a decent living standard were possible for them if they worked hard and played by the rules. This belief is at the heart of the American dream.

The problem, however, is that for many, upward mobility has become more dream than reality. Discrimination, be it based on race, gender, ethnicity, religion, sexual orientation, age, or something else, persists and blocks opportunity. But inequality of opportunity goes beyond specific acts of discrimination and also reflects unequal access to quality education and other resources, financial and otherwise.

Economic insecurity is widespread. Middle-class incomes remained stagnant in real terms for decades. Factories closed and jobs disappeared, largely on account of new technologies that increased productivity, though trade pacts often unfairly bore the blame. Insecurity of another kind is also a factor, as a good many Americans are uncomfortable with cultural and demographic trends that they believe are leading to a loss of work and status.

Americans increasingly feel disillusioned with and alienated from their government and their country. The 2007–2008 financial crisis, in large part brought about by insufficient regulation of economic activity and mortgages in particular, contributed to a lack of confidence in government and a loss of belief that average Americans can affect it. There is a perception, reinforced by reality, that the political system is unresponsive to addressing many of the country's most pressing ills, including the poor and uneven quality of public education, infrastructure, climate change, debt, the opioid crisis, policing, and a dysfunctional healthcare system. It comes as little surprise that in a recent poll only 57 percent of young people age eighteen to twenty-nine said it was very important that the country is a democracy. Foreign policy has a role here as well, in that some of the most costly decisions—in human and economic terms—made by the government involved what I have described as wars of choice, conflicts where American soldiers were sent to fight where U.S. interests were not vital or where other policy options existed. Here I would list the Vietnam War as well as the decisions to intervene militarily in Iraq in 2003 and to significantly expand the limited intervention begun in Afghanistan in late 2001. The fact that no weapons of mass destruction were ever found in Iraq, the ostensible rationale for the war, fed mistrust of government and elites. That the Taliban regained power after two decades of failed but costly effort in Afghanistan likewise raised doubts about government competence.

Another factor is the weakening of what political scientists term "intermediary institutions," namely those that occupy the space between voters and those in power. It is the political analogue to what has happened in parts of the economy, where businesses that managed ties between individuals and other businesses (as, say, travel agencies did with airlines and hotels) have been bypassed by technologies that allow individuals to deal directly with those whose services they seek. National political parties have not disappeared, but they have become weaker and less important. Decades ago, the Democratic and Republican parties were moderating influences in that they had enormous influence over who could stand for office and who could draw on their resources for elections. This led to tight control over what positions and policies could be embraced by individual members of Congress. Now, however, every candidate or elected politician is increasingly his or her own political party, able to reach voters and sources of money directly without having to depend on parties. More and more, such sources of funds are national in scope. Extremism tends to be rewarded as the most active participants in the political process are often those with narrow concerns that are intensely felt. This explains why, as noted earlier, even modest efforts to control firearms rarely succeed even though polls indicate a majority of Americans favor such controls. The same holds for the inability to pass trade legislation even though a majority of Americans support trade. Intense minorities often overwhelm more restrained majorities in the political marketplace. Compromise and even civility tend to be seen as a sign of weakness. The center has been hollowed out.

Technology plays a role in explaining how we arrived where we are. I grew up at a time when there were three television networks. FM radio was in its infancy, while satellite radio did not exist. Nor did personal computers, much less the Internet. Television, the dominant media of the era, tended to bring the country together, as it was a source of shared experience. The situation today could hardly be more different. There are thousands of television stations, at least as many radio stations, and countless websites, blogs, and podcasts that are essentially broadcasters and publishers. Social media is especially pernicious, as it tends to undermine social trust, weaken institutions, and create mini-societies with their own narratives. We have moved from broadcasting to narrowcasting. Choice is effectively unlimited, and many gravitate to outlets that reflect not just their interests but their biases. Missing is any quality control. Misinformation is rampant, balance rarely found. Algorithms that direct a person to content that reinforces existing beliefs, in the process hardening views and increasing division, are widespread; antisocial media might be a more apt term. The end result is that we have a near unlimited number of venues with few gatekeepers.

The result is a society defined by a lack of shared experiences. A frequent debate when I was growing up in the 1960s was between America as a melting pot, in which Americanness would overwhelm all else, and a mixing pot, in which differences relating to color or religion or country of origin would be maintained within a single society. Today, American society is less a melting or mixing pot than a loose collection of separate pots. We are not so much members of a single large society as multiple smaller societies, defined by geography, political beliefs, religion (or, as is increasingly the case, a lack of one), color, educational attainment, and class. As former Court of Appeals Judge J. Michael Luttig stated before the January 6 committee, "We Americans no longer agree on what is right or wrong, what is to be valued and what is not, what is acceptable behavior and not, and what is and is not tolerable discourse in civilized society."

There is a clustering or sorting within society that reflects choice but also a lack of mobility and a lack of mechanisms, such as the draft, that involved Americans from all walks of life in common endeavors.

Adding to the lack of national community is that none of what is essential for a democracy to thrive is automatically passed on from generation to generation. To the contrary, it needs to be taught, including its history, values, and obligations. There is no accepted national curriculum. It is impossible to preserve a system that is not widely understood or valued.

Something of a cottage industry has grown up around what to do to fix things. Even a partial list would include providing greater protection for voting rights along with arrangements (including making Election Day a federal holiday) that make it easier to vote; making voting mandatory; introducing a voter identification requirement; ending the gerrymandering of congressional and state legislative districts, especially when it reduces the number of districts that are truly competitive or where centrists stand a chance; public financing of political campaigns; revising the Electoral Count Act of 1877 to limit the discretion of the Congress, the vice president, and state governors in determining delegations sent by states to the electoral college; making Washington, D.C., a state; increasing regulation of social media to hold social media companies responsible for content that incites violence or is patently false; reintroducing some version of the "fairness doctrine" so that media are required to put forward alternative points of view; ending so-called dark money donations in political campaigns; establishing open primaries in which party membership is not a prerequisite for voting; introducing ranked-choice voting; making it less difficult for a third-party candidate to participate in presidential debates; creating a new, centrist political party; reining in the use of the filibuster in the Senate; limiting or getting rid of "holds" by which individual senators can prevent votes on specific nominations; expanding the size of the House of Representatives; introducing term limits on judges, members of Congress, and other elected officials; expanding the number of Supreme Court justices; convening a constitutional convention; encouraging young adults to perform one or two years of national service; and mandating civics education.

In a similar vein, there are many proposals in circulation as to what could and should be done to improve the economic situation of many Americans. Some of these fall under the rubric of transfer payments: guaranteeing a baseline income through the provision of a universal basic income; subsidized childcare; universal pre-K education; child tax credits; expanded health insurance coverage; paid family leave; free or reduced-cost community college; and college loan forgiveness. Other policy proposals in this realm tend to emphasize tax reform: higher tax rates on individual income or corporate profits; reducing or ending the separate, preferential tax treatment of capital gains; treating carried interest as normal income for tax purposes; introducing taxes on wealth above designated levels; much more stringent limits on intergenerational transfers of wealth through higher inheritance taxes or other laws. Also, there are calls for means-testing benefits, expanding foreign trade, and both increasing and curtailing immigration.

Again, many readers will have their own ideas. We might be better off if some or even many of these changes came to pass. But few are likely to, in no small part because the same problems that have led to the weakening of democracy here make it difficult to fix it. It is not just that the process of reform is arduous; it is more that those who perceive the changes would restrain their rights will oppose them. This is where obligations come in: American democracy will work and reform will prove possible only if obligations join rights at center stage.

PART TWO

——

THE BILL OF OBLIGATIONS

——

OBLIGATION I

Be Informed

The belief that an informed citizenry is essential to the survival of American democracy is as old as the republic itself. Thomas Jefferson emphasized the link, pointing out that "wherever the people are well informed they can be trusted with their own government; that whenever things get so far wrong as to attract their notice, they may be relied on to set them to rights." Some two centuries later, the forty-fourth president, Barack Obama, made a similar point, arguing that "This democracy doesn't work if we don't have an informed citizenry."

All of which raises a few questions: What is an informed citizenry? Why is it so important? And what does it take to become and stay an informed citizen?

First things first. An informed citizen is someone who understands the fundamentals as to how the government and the economy and society operate, the principal challenges facing the country at home and abroad, and the contending options or policies for dealing with those challenges. An informed citizen is someone who puts himself or herself in a position to weigh what others say or write and contribute their own perspectives. Ideally, this individual would also know something of the country's history and how it came to be what it is today, as it is impossible to understand the present without an appreciation of the past. History also provides lessons for contemporary challenges.

Why is an informed citizenry essential? American democracy is a representative (rather than direct) democracy, in which citizens do not make day-to-day decisions as to what the federal, state, or local government should do with its powers and resources but rather elect individuals to do just that. It is thus a republic; in the words of James Madison, "a government which derives all its powers directly or indirectly from the great body of the people, and is administered by persons holding their offices during pleasure, for a limited period, or during good behavior."

The obvious reason, then, for citizens to be informed is to be able to wisely cast their votes. In almost every instance there are two or more candidates vying for a position, and it is in your self-interest to know enough to determine which of the candidates would be likely to advance or support policies you judge to be desirable. Implicit in this decision is knowing not simply what a candidate stands for but also the likely consequences of the policies they stand for and oppose so that you are in a position to determine what policy choices make the most sense.

Related to this is the importance of holding officials accountable. Reelection is something to be earned, not a right. And between elections there are other avenues to affect the behavior of elected officials, above all by shaping the context in which they operate. Few public officials want to alienate voters, and organizing rallies and protests, contacting the office of your representative or senator, asking questions at candidate forums, contributing money, and otherwise supporting groups dedicated to particular political outcomes can have a meaningful impact.

Being informed also empowers individuals to have influence over positions the business or organization they work for might take. Or to shape the views of the people in their lives.

By contrast, an uninformed citizenry constitutes a risk to democracy. Those who are uninformed are less likely to be involved if for no other reason than it is difficult to motivate yourself to vote if it is not clear why it is worth it. And an uninformed citizenry is much more vulnerable to being misled by falsehoods and unfounded conspiracy theories or manipulated by politicians who are pursuing their personal interests.

Where does one go to become or remain an informed citizen? In principle, it should be easy, as we are living in an age in which accurate information is more accessible than ever before in human history. In practice, though, it is anything but, as misinformation is just as abundant as the facts. As a result, becoming an informed citizen is not easy. I suggested earlier that becoming an informed citizen begins with understanding how the government operates. This is the material that ought to be taught in every school in the country. Outside of school, the basics can still be gleaned from a reading of the country's founding documents and a handful of books. What comes to mind are the Declaration of Independence, the Constitution, and *The Federalist Papers*, along with the best biographies and speeches of major presidents as well as some respected histories and commentaries, such as Alexis de Tocqueville's *Democracy in America*. In the "Where to Go for More" section at the end of this book, I have listed some of my favorite books dealing with this country's past and politics. The wisdom in these texts is evergreen, especially since the information they pass along to a reader changes slowly, if at all.

The same cannot be said for issue-related content, which changes all the time. Remaining up to speed requires constant effort, ideally on a daily basis, or, failing that, weekly. There is also no one-stop shopping when it comes to this information; indeed, a principle ought to be that every citizen seeks out more than one source given that any single source is inevitably biased in what it covers or how it covers it. That said, all sources are not equal, and any citizen would do well to read a major newspaper such as the *New York Times*, *Wall Street Journal*, *Washington Post*, and others that have bureaus around the world and cover global developments. Smaller newspapers that cannot afford national and international bureaus or staffs of their own can still provide useful coverage of local issues. What traditional newspapers have in common is that they have fact-checkers and editors, and they make an effort—admittedly not always successful—to separate the political biases of the paper from the news coverage. There are several quality weekly and monthly magazines and political newsletters, which are also discussed in the "Where to Go for More" section. Public radio and television offer serious coverage of domestic and international news. The nightly news broadcasts on the networks offer some news, the network morning shows less.

We live in a world shaped by a large and growing number of AM, FM, and satellite radio shows; cable and network television channels; podcasts; social media platforms such as Facebook, Twitter, and Instagram; websites; and more that often have a narrow or biased take on events and seek to reinforce the views and biases of their select audience. Seek out a range of sources and choose those that traffic in facts rather than falsehoods and conspiracies. Social media can be especially problematic, as people choose communities or follow only those who are like-minded. Misstatements and opinions are often presented as facts when they are anything but. It is not research to visit such sites and accept what they say as gospel.

Given all of this, how do we know when a fact is a fact? It is essential to differentiate among facts, misstatements, opinions, predictions, and recommendations. Facts are assertions that can be demonstrated to be so, measured, and proved. Misstatements are assertions that can be shown to be false or inaccurate. For the record, there are no alternative facts, just facts and misstatements. Opinions are judgments or assessments, often suggesting why something took place along with its consequences. They must be made from or based on the relevant facts—not just those that fit a certain preference—if they are to hold value. But even then they are not to be equated with facts. Predictions are statements about the future and how it is likely to turn out. Recommendations are statements of preferences about what should be done about a certain problem or situation.

For example: It is a fact that the national debt of the United States is approximately $31 trillion. To say anything else is a misstatement. But to argue that a debt of this scale is something that is dangerous and ought to be reduced, or is something that can safely be maintained, is a matter of analysis. To say the debt will increase to a certain level by a certain date is a prediction. To argue that the debt should be reduced through increased taxation or reduced spending is a recommendation. Informed and reasonable people can and do disagree on everything but the basic facts. The reasons for their different views might reflect assumptions about future economic growth or interest rates or policy priorities. What is clear, though, is that a productive debate over how to view the debt and what, if anything, to do about it can occur only if the debate is based on a common set of facts as to its size.

Or take climate change. That the temperature of the atmosphere has increased 1.1 degrees centigrade (approximately two degrees Fahrenheit) since the onset of the industrial age is a fact. A widely shared assessment is that this temperature increase stems overwhelmingly from human activity and that it has resulted in more frequent and more violent storms, floods, fires, and droughts. That the temperature will increase by an additional half a degree centigrade (about a degree Fahrenheit) over the next decade is a prediction. And then to advocate for greater use of renewable fuels and nuclear power and reduced use of fossil fuels are recommendations, as are calls for greater regulation or taxation of carbon emissions.

The COVID-19 pandemic likewise provides multiple illustrations of what is being discussed here. It is a fact that as of summer 2022 at least one million Americans and fifteen to twenty million people worldwide have died of complications stemming from COVID-19. To deny this is to misstate what has occurred. To say that the virus emerged accidentally from a laboratory in Wuhan, China, is an assessment; to say it emerged from so-called wet markets in China is a competing assessment. To project that millions more will die from the virus or one of its variants is a prediction. It is a fact that vaccination and the wearing of masks can protect people from infection and save lives; to argue that the federal, state, or city governments ought to mandate either of these actions is a policy recommendation.

What comes to mind here is a famous statement attributed to Daniel Patrick Moynihan, the former Harvard professor, adviser to President Richard Nixon, and senator from New York, who noted that "everyone is entitled to his own opinion, but not to his own facts." Or more recently, the head of the Associated Press made the following statement: "COVID vaccines are safe. Climate change is real. There was no widespread fraud in the [2020] U.S. election. Those are not political positions; those are fact-based positions." Or as then Fox News correspondent Chris Wallace put it, "Truth is non-negotiable. There's no spin to truth. Truth is truth." Meaningful debate, much less the development of sound policy, is impossible if it is not rooted in facts.

Behind each of those statements is a mountain of evidence that withstands scrutiny. COVID vaccines have been administered to billions with only a handful of side effects. That the earth's temperature has gone up by some two degrees Fahrenheit since the start of the industrial revolution is measurable and has in fact been measured. The 2020 presidential election has been the subject of some sixty investigations or audits at the state level and the results show that nothing occurred in the voting or counting of votes that materially affected the election outcome.

All three of these assertions of fact are rejected by some. Distinguishing between facts and misstatements is not always easy, and judging the quality of analyses, predictions, and recommendations can be even more difficult. One has to look at the source, the degree of expert backing and their confidence in what is asserted, and what they point to as evidence in order to justify their level of confidence. For example, it is significant when almost all the leading experts in the field are able to explain why they are

99 percent confident in a proposition, and an opposing position is backed by a handful of people with few relevant credentials who cannot justify their stance. In the case of climate change, for example, it is worth mentioning that the August 2021 UN report that presented climate-related science in great detail was supported by 234 of the leading experts in the world and over fourteen thousand authoritative studies. With analysis it is important to take note of the factual foundation (or lack of it) as well as the rationale provided for conclusions reached. Similarly, it is important to look at what lies behind predictions. Recommendations should always come with an assessment of likely costs and benefits as well as predictions of impact. I have a rule of thumb when it comes to assessments: if you have to cook the books to make your argument, if you have to avoid inconvenient truths or manufacture others, it may be time to reconsider your position.

Experts can be wrong at times, as most were in stating that Iraq had weapons of mass destruction in the run-up to the 2003 war. This proved to be a misstatement. There is a distinction, though, between misstatements based on a faulty assessment of available evidence (which this proved to be) and those made with intent, i.e., lies, in which known facts are ignored or material is presented as fact when it is not. What experts owe the public in such cases is not just their rigorous analysis but also statements of how confident they are in their assessments and how they came to them.

The point being made here is not that understanding what is and is not a fact will lead to agreement, which it most surely will not, but rather that it will provide the basis for productive debate and, in the end, wiser policy. It will also protect individuals from those who would mislead them, to better advocate for what is in their self-interest, and to put them in a position to hold those with power to account. Getting and staying informed takes time and energy, but the results for individuals and the country make it worthwhile.

When it comes to our obligation to be informed, those in the position to influence the views of others have a special responsibility to get their facts right and to distinguish carefully among facts, assessments, predictions, and recommendations. This applies to teachers at every level, to those who give sermons in places of worship, to journalists and those in every type of media, and above all to those in government, be they elected or appointed, who possess not just influence but power. For good reason the Old and New Testament alike make the case that to whom much is given, much is required.

OBLIGATION II

Get Involved

A democracy depends on the participation of its citizens. It is rule *by* the people rather than *of* the people. Yes, in a representative democracy elected and appointed officials wield a great deal of power, but the point is that this power is derived from those who elect them and give them the power to act. The Declaration of Independence explicitly makes this point: "Governments are instituted among men, deriving their just powers from the consent of the governed."

This all requires, though, that citizens take an active part in their democracy. It may seem hard to believe that they would not, in that people fought and died for the American colonies to become an independent, democratic country not subjugated to a king or to a parliament they had no influence over. But in fact many Americans do not participate actively in their democracy.

It is ironic that we have gone to war for the right of others to be free but all too often seem content not to take advantage of the reality that we are.

The most basic measure of democratic involvement is voting. Yet over the past fifty years, approximately one-third to 40 percent of eligible voters have failed to vote in U.S. presidential elections— and over half do not vote in midterm elections for congressional or state and local candidates. For comparison, one recent survey of thirty-five democracies with successful economies showed the United States ranked thirtieth when it came to the percentage of the voting-age population that actually voted.

The reasons people give for not voting are many: not being registered to vote, being uninterested in politics, not liking any of the choices, not getting time off from work, a sense their vote would not make a difference. These explanations demonstrate that many citizens feel alienation from, and a lack of trust in, a political process that they believe is rigged in favor of the rich and powerful or those harboring opposing political perspectives; that some have made the judgment that the outcome of an election will not affect their lives in ways that matter; and that others perceive the process as too time-consuming and too difficult given their other priorities.

It is easy to see how people might conclude their vote doesn't matter when it is just one vote of more than 150 million cast in a presidential election. This calculation, however, misses the reality that, due to the electoral college, a presidential election is not so much a single national election as fifty state elections. The voters in each state cast their ballots, and under the winner-take-all system in all but two states (Maine and Nebraska) 100 percent of that state's electoral votes go to the candidate who wins the most votes in that state. It doesn't matter how many votes a candidate receives or that they achieve a majority. All it takes to receive all of a state's electoral votes is for a candidate to receive more votes than anyone else. The number of electoral votes for any state represents the number of seats allocated to the state in the House of Representatives plus the two senate seats each state enjoys regardless of population. Electoral votes thus range from a minimum of three (in the case of low-population states such as Wyoming, Alaska, and a handful of others) to California's fifty-five. As we have seen five times in U.S. history, including the 2016 presidential election, it is possible to be elected president with a majority of the electoral votes but receive fewer overall votes than your opponent. In perhaps the starkest example, in Florida in 2000, George W. Bush defeated Al Gore by 537 votes out of nearly six million cast. And it was Florida's electoral votes that handed Bush the presidency.

Outcomes have been even closer in other races. In 2008, the U.S. Senate race in Minnesota—in which the Democratic candidate Al Franken defeated the Republican Norm Coleman—was decided by just 312 votes out of nearly three million cast. The result gave Democrats enough of a margin in the Senate to overcome Republican attempts to block legislation. Then, in 2017, an election for the Virginia House of Delegates ended in a tie. The winner was chosen by picking a name out of a glass bowl. What is more, it was this election that gave Republicans control of the House of Delegates by a single seat. In the future, such control of state legislatures could have an impact not just on issues germane to the state but to presidential elections if there is a debate over the accuracy and legitimacy of voting and the delegates to be sent to the electoral college.

What happened in the small New Hampshire town of Croydon is instructive here. At a sparsely attended town meeting in March 2022, a handful of activists passed an amendment that slashed the town's education budget. Most of the townspeople were dismayed when they heard the news, but their only recourse was to convene a second special meeting at which half the eligible voters would need to turn out and vote to restore the cuts. Following weeks of intense efforts to educate and motivate the townspeople, an overwhelming majority of voters did just that in May. What matters in a democracy is not the views of a majority of the populace but those of a majority willing to get involved politically.

In short, voting matters. But the reasons voting is so important and is worth doing go beyond the potential of a single vote to affect election outcomes, which admittedly is rare. Voting is the most basic act of citizenship. It creates a bond between the individual and government and between the individual and country. It gives an individual standing in the political arena: criticism carries more weight when someone is a participant in the political process. Ideally, the process of voting increases awareness of issues and what is at stake and thus motivates people to be better informed. It provides a mechanism for individuals to influence the political process and creates a basis for them to hold accountable those elected and appointed since they had a role in choosing them. Voting is so intrinsic to democracy's success that several democratic countries, including Australia and Belgium, legally require their citizens to vote.

As fundamental and important as it is, however, voting is hardly the only form of meaningful political participation. Even a short list of other aspects of the democratic process might include encouraging fellow citizens to register and vote and educating them on the issues, working for a party or candidate, assisting the local board of elections in administering the voting process and the counting of votes, and contributing money to the candidate, party, or cause of your choice.

There are many other ways to bolster democracy beyond voting and direct involvement in politics. What is more, you need not be famous or powerful to make a difference. As former Secretary of Defense James Mattis pointed out, "The impact of participation trickles up. Rosa Parks didn't start out by taking on all of Jim Crow; she started out by taking a seat on a local bus." A group of parents initiated what turned out to be a successful recall of three members of San Francisco's school board in 2022. One woman, after losing a family member in an automobile accident, came up with the idea that became Mothers Against Drunk Driving (MADD), an organization that over the past four decades has saved countless lives. Or take gerrymandering, the process by which the majority party in a state legislature draws the lines of congressional or state legislative districts in an attempt to disadvantage the minority party. (A second consequence of gerrymandering is to increase extremism, as districts tend to be dominated by one or the other party, thereby reducing the need for candidates to attract votes from the political center in order to build a majority.) In Michigan, the entire process was turned around by a woman with no political experience who in the wake of the 2016 election used social media to launch a volunteer movement that took the power to draw districts from the state government and awarded it to an independent commission.

Parents have an especially important role to play: they have both the responsibility and the opportunity to encourage their children to learn about and get involved in the political process. In recent months, we have seen parents at school board meetings arguing, sometimes violently, over how race is treated in school curricula. Alas, we are not seeing much in the way of parental involvement on behalf of including democracy in what schools teach their students. Ronald Reagan put it best in his farewell address delivered in 1989: "All great change in America begins at the dinner table. So, tomorrow night in the kitchen I hope the talking begins. . . . That would be a very American thing to do."

Corporate leaders also have the opportunity to become advocates for democracy. At a minimum, they can facilitate time off to vote on election day for all employees. Ideally, they would determine their financial contributions to candidates not just on grounds of policy but also based on the person's support for democracy. Better yet, they would also refuse to advertise on media outlets that trafficked in misinformation and conspiracies. Employees can press their bosses to do all this. So, too, can investors and consumers of the company's products and services.

Similarly, religious and congregational leaders possess meaningful influence. Nearly half of adult Americans regularly attend a religious service, which, even allowing for distraction and nodding off, adds up to a good many sermons and homilies from the pulpit being heard by a good many people. I appreciate how it can be difficult for the clergy to advocate for particular policy prescriptions, but there is much in the teachings found in the Old and New Testaments and in other religious works consistent with many of the obligations put forward here. The clergy have regular opportunities to point this out.

The message that runs through this obligation is that democracy cannot be a spectator sport. Passivity and opting out simply allow others to choose for you, which almost certainly means advancing their preferences rather than your own. Given how much is at stake, it is hard to defend inaction. It is better to vote in favor of candidates who reflect your views than not to vote but attend political rallies protesting outcomes you oppose. The case for getting involved and remaining involved is overwhelming. Democracy is a form of government that empowers individual citizens—but only if citizens are prepared to get involved.

OBLIGATION III

Stay Open to Compromise

I am not sure when "compromise" became a four-letter word. (For the record, it is ten.) For some, it is little more than a synonym for selling out, for abandoning one's principles in pursuit of an outcome. The nineteenth-century industrialist Andrew Carnegie is reported to have said that "compromise is usually a sign of weakness, or an admission of defeat." When John Boehner, the Speaker of the House from 2011 to 2015, was asked about compromise during an interview on *60 Minutes*, he said, "I reject the word." Implicit in this view is that what is given away is more valuable than what was gained. Also implicit is that the motive for someone accepting such an outcome is unflattering, that it represents the pursuit of something impure or ill-advised or misguided.

John F. Kennedy, however, made the case for compromise: "Compromise need not mean cowardice. Indeed it is frequently the compromisers and conciliators who are faced with the severest tests of political courage as they oppose the extremist views of their constituents."

Compromise was at the heart of the process that led to the Constitution. Alexander Hamilton recognized that "the compacts which are to embrace thirteen distinct states in a common bond of amity and union must as necessarily be a compromise of as many dissimilar interests and inclinations." The differing interests of small- and large-population states were accommodated in the so-called Great Compromise, where representation in one chamber of Congress—the Senate—was made the same for all states and the other—the House of Representatives—contingent on population. Centuries later, Wyoming and California each have two senators, but California has fifty-three representatives to Wyoming's one. There were other compromises, including that of 1790, by which the federal government took over state debts, advocated by Alexander Hamilton, in exchange for moving the new country's capital from New York to Washington, D.C., something sought by Thomas Jefferson. And last but far from least, the agreement to adopt ten amendments to the new Constitution, what became known as the Bill of Rights, was itself a compromise between advocates of a strong central government and those who feared it and insisted on these protections and guarantees as a condition of signing on.

If, however, compromise was once as American as apple pie,

it is no longer. This is a serious problem. I've put forth compromise as an obligation because it is essential to getting things done in any situation in which power is distributed among multiple sets of hands, which is the case in a democracy. Henry Clay, a mentor of Abraham Lincoln and a Speaker of the House of Representatives known as the "great compromiser" for his role in putting together a set of legislative initiatives that effectively delayed the Civil War, put it best: "All legislation, all government, all society is founded upon the principle of mutual concession." Compromise is the process by which all relevant parties are incentivized to go along with an alternative arrangement. An all-or-nothing approach to bargaining will almost always result in the latter.

But compromise has virtues other than as a means to the end of reaching agreement when parties disagree. It can create a foundation on top of which additional measures can be added over time. An agreement born of compromise can be understood as the first, not the last, act of a play. As Ronald Reagan noted in his autobiography, "If you got 75 or 80 percent of what you were asking for, I say, you take it and fight for the rest later, and that's what I told these radical conservatives who never got used to it." Reagan also reflected, "They wanted all or nothing and they wanted it all at once."

Compromise also broadens the degree and range of political support for what is agreed to. This can be essential for big initiatives. It is almost always a mistake to enact big changes in a democracy without broad support. Such support means an outcome is less likely to be successfully attacked and less likely to be gutted or scrapped if and when the political winds change and those who opposed the deal find themselves in positions of power. It is debatable whether Republicans were prepared to support the expansion of healthcare to millions of Americans as was done under the Affordable Care Act (aka "Obamacare") over 2009 and 2010; that said, the fact that such important legislation was passed by one party alone—unlike, say, Medicare in 1965—left the initiative far more vulnerable. It is ironic, and frustrating, that so many laud bipartisanship but seem to overlook that it requires compromise if it is to produce results.

The importance of compromise leading to broad support can be especially important in foreign policy, where a lack of predictability and consistency can undermine alliances, as countries that put their security in America's hands must be confident that we will come to their defense in a crisis. American instability will also tempt foes to be more bellicose, as they will sense opportunity more than risk. It is quite possible that such a calculation entered into Vladimir Putin's decision to launch a war against Ukraine in February 2022. Refusing to compromise has also led presidents to forge international agreements on their own that could not muster bipartisan support in the Congress.

President Barack Obama chose to sign an agreement in 2015 limiting Iran's nuclear activities (in exchange for which Iran received significant economic benefits) without formal congressional involvement. This lack of congressional approval made it both possible and easy for President Obama to enter into the pact—but also possible and easy for his successor, Donald Trump, to unilaterally exit the agreement three years later. This inconsistency hurt America's credibility as a negotiating partner and strained its relationships with its allies, which depend on American constancy. It has also complicated efforts to negotiate a new agreement with Iran, which has expressed concerns that commitments made by the Biden administration might not be honored by its successor. An alternative approach would have been to submit the accord as a treaty, something that would have been difficult to gain approval for, as a treaty requires approval by two-thirds of the senators present when it comes up for a vote. There was also the option of submitting the agreement with Iran to the Congress in the form of a so-called executive agreement, which would have required only a majority vote in both the Senate and the House of Representatives. Whatever the approach, the same process would have been required to extricate the United States from its commitments, thereby making it unlikely the Trump administration could have withdrawn when and how it did. Again, there is an obvious trade-off between getting what you want and having it survive. The question is whether the compromises that would be required to get it approved (and that would lock it in) are acceptable.

Compromise inevitably involves risk. There will always be those who opt for purity over progress. They will insist that any compromise is a sellout. The flaw in such thinking is that what from their perspective is necessary is not achievable. As the adage goes, half a loaf is better than none. This was exactly the thinking of those proponents of gun control (or enhanced public safety) who in the wake of multiple mass-casualty shootings in 2022 agreed to support legislation that did not include many of the provisions they judged desirable. Interestingly, on the other side were opponents of any constraints who feared they would only pave the way to more severe limits. Legislation that introduced modest new constraints passed Congress only when the absolutists on both sides of the debate were outnumbered by a majority who came together to reflect the public desire for at least some action.

There is such a thing as too great a willingness to compromise. This was the case with British foreign policy in the years before World War II, where concessions were made time and again in what proved to be a futile effort to avert war with Nazi Germany. The policy of appeasement gave compromise a bad name. The lesson is not to always reject compromise, but to be sure that what is gained is equal to or greater than what is given up. It is also necessary to ask what is likely to follow. In this case, the desire for peace at any price ultimately turned out to be more costly than resistance. Much the same logic has led Ukraine's president, Volodymyr Zelenskyy, to reject calls for compromise that would leave Russia in control of a significant portion of Ukraine's territory.

When is it right to compromise—and when to stand firm? A

basic rule of thumb is to hold fast on matters of fundamental principle; Mahatma Gandhi, the advocate of nonviolence who led India's movement for independence from Great Britain, is reported to have said that "all compromise is based on give and take, but there can be no give and take on fundamentals. Any compromise on mere fundamentals is a surrender. For it is all give and no take."

How do we discern what is fundamental and what is secondary or even peripheral? In many instances what is fundamental is to establish something, be it a program or an agreement. There is still room for compromise when it comes to accepting a deal that includes only some of what was desired. There is as well flexibility with regard to the details of the scale of what is put forward or required, the scope, and the pace and sequencing of implementation. Over time the scale can be expanded or the scope extended. In some situations, there may be reason to compromise in order to make it possible for the other side to sell what is being negotiated to its own base.

One way to think about compromise is as a choice. What are the likely pros and cons of agreeing to a deal that could be reached (rather than some idyllic but impossible to reach pact)—compared with the pros and cons of not having a deal? In the world of negotiation this is sometimes referred to as your best alternative to a negotiated agreement. There is in principle a third option, a better deal, but at some point in every negotiation that option disappears as the other party decides it is better off without a deal than with giving in more. Which brings you back to the deal that can be negotiated versus not having one.

Such calculations were at work in what was arguably the most famous compromise of the modern era, namely, the one that ended the Cuban Missile Crisis in 1962. The Soviet decision to install nuclear-armed missiles in Cuba that could reach the continental United States in just a few minutes brought the two superpowers to the brink of nuclear war as President John F. Kennedy declared this to be unacceptable. After a tense few days, Soviet leader Nikita Khrushchev backed down and agreed to withdraw the missiles—but only when President Kennedy agreed not to invade Cuba and secretly assured Khrushchev he would withdraw from Turkey medium-range missiles capable of reaching the Soviet Union. The concessions were judged acceptable by both sides in order to avoid a nuclear war that would be devastating for both.

Compromise almost always leaves the individual doing the compromise vulnerable, especially in political primaries, which in most states include voters in only a single party and tend to bring out only the most motivated and ideological. Voters in turn are influenced by special interest groups, which focus all their resources on one issue or set of issues and often reject all compromise without regard to other aspects of the issue or other issues and relationships. Compromise also leaves one vulnerable to criticism in the media. The narrowness of many radio and cable audiences all but ensures anyone who compromises will be criticized on grounds that too little was achieved or too much given up or on the precedent established.

There is no way to prevent such criticism. Compromise has to be defended and explained. It is never enough in public life to do the right thing, as important as that is. It is just as important to explain and educate as to why it was the right thing to do and better than any available alternative. I, for one, thought that President George H. W. Bush was right to violate his "Read my lips: no new taxes" pledge in 1990 in order to reach a budget deal with sufficient bipartisan support; where I think he erred was in not explaining to the American people why this was the right thing to do for the country. It is a good lesson—namely, that those willing to compromise must take the time and make the effort to explain why it was desirable to do so and left citizens better off than they would otherwise have been.

OBLIGATION IV

Remain Civil

Civility and being civil to others are essential to the workings of democracy.

Civility is closely aligned with manners. With respect. With courtesy. With politeness. To learn how to disagree without being disagreeable. To paraphrase the Golden Rule, civility is about treating others as you would like others to treat you.

At least two former presidents have weighed in on the word. John F. Kennedy, in his famous "Ask not what your country can do for you—ask what you can do for your country" inaugural address, noted that "civility is not a sign of weakness." Forty years later, in his first inaugural address, George W. Bush expressed it this way: "Civility is not a tactic or a sentiment; it is the determined choice of trust over cynicism, of community over chaos."

Why is this concept so important? Disagreements are inevitable in a democracy. Opinions often are strong or even emotional. The subject can be anything, be it public spending, taxes, race, gender, political and personal rights, abortion, guns, masks, vaccinations, arrangements for voting or the counting of ballots, or matters of war and peace. What civility does is make it possible for differences to be reduced or even bridged—and even if not, civility allows for dialogue and relationships to continue on other issues where agreement might not be out of the question. Opponents on one issue need not become opponents on all issues, much less enemies. Civility greatly decreases the chances that disagreements will spill over into violence.

How can civility be promoted? It is best to deal with issues and arguments on their merits, not on motives you might ascribe to those making the arguments. For starters, there is no way of knowing how or why someone came to the position he or she is advocating. We come to hold certain beliefs and preferences for multiple, complex reasons that reflect our experiences, background, associations, education, ambitions, prejudices, and more. In many cases, these motivations may be unknown even to us. For these and other reasons it is far more productive to just deal with the arguments and issues at hand, not with what you imagine lies behind them.

There is also a case to avoid making things personal. It may be possible to find common ground on issues, but it will quickly become impossible to do so when the issue becomes the other person's motives, character, or intelligence. Ad hominem attacks and derogatory labels make people defensive and angry, which hardly increases their willingness to compromise or even listen to what you are saying.

Tone matters. Volume rarely improves the quality of an argument. The same can be said for repetition. Similarly, it can help to ask the other person to state not just his or her bottom line but the thinking behind it. Avoid characterizing the other person's argument in loaded terms: "racist" or "sexist" or "stupid." Here it can also help to repeat what you understand to be the stance of the other person or group and ask them if you have it right. It can also help to ask questions as to how they arrived at a certain position or whether they are in principle open to anything less than what they are advocating. Coming to appreciate what it is to walk in the other person's shoes can be invaluable.

It can be extraordinarily difficult to remain civil in the face of pronounced incivility, in particular when someone verbally attacks you. My advice in such circumstances is to respond calmly—doing so tends to make the other person look even worse and turns off others who might otherwise be attracted to their stance—and either ignore the comments or end the conversation on the grounds that their prejudice makes further exchanges unproductive. To be civil toward someone does not signal a lack of conviction or principle on your part. It does not signal a willingness to compromise, although compromise, as I've discussed, is often required for democracy to work.

It bears saying that the purpose of conversations is not to demolish the other side; political disagreement is not a high school or college debating tournament. Humiliation turns out to be a powerful motive in human behavior, and those who feel humiliated or talked down to will dig in or even seek revenge. It doesn't cost you anything to treat someone else with dignity even if you believe they are unworthy of it or that their arguments have little or no merit.

A politically charged conversation can also be a moment to learn. One purpose of conversation and debate is to better understand the issues and the considerations associated with them. It can help you hone your own arguments to reduce the resistance to them or increase the odds that what you want will be accepted and implemented. And at the risk of being called naive, there is even the chance that civil argument and disagreement will persuade you to change your mind.

Speaking of changing one's mind, as is the case with civility and compromise, doing so is no sign of weakness. I am reminded of the quote often attributed to the great twentieth-century British economist John Maynard Keynes, who when challenged on just this, is said to have quipped, "When the facts change, I change my mind. What do you do, sir?" Changing one's mind can be a sign of strength and wisdom, especially if new facts emerge or if what were thought to be facts are shown to be otherwise. To stand fast in light of new compelling evidence or argument is simply to be stubborn and to adopt a stance that blocks reaching common ground.

Unfortunately, we are living in a time rife with a lack of civility. I can still see President Trump standing behind the podium in the House of Representatives, about to deliver his annual State of the Union address to the Congress and the American people. The custom is that before doing so he gives a copy of the speech to the vice president and the Speaker of the House of Representatives (each of whom sits behind him) and shakes their hands in the process. In this case the president refused to shake Speaker Nancy Pelosi's hand; not to be outdone, the Speaker of the House ostentatiously ripped the speech in half after the president had read it. That two of the most powerful figures in the country had descended to such a level reveals much.

Or more recently there was the incident in which Senator Kyrsten Sinema of Arizona was followed into the ladies room by a group of individuals angry with her over her stance on immigration reform. As my mother used to say, there is a time and place for everything, and shouting at someone behind the door of a bathroom stall is neither the time nor place for such an interaction. The same holds for protesting outside the homes of Supreme Court justices when they are associated with an unpopular opinion. I would add that such behavior hardly wins converts to the cause.

How did we get to such a point? I am not sure I have a good

answer to that question. One thing I do know is that social media both contributes to the coarsening of our discourse and reflects it. Spend five minutes on Twitter and it is next to impossible not to be taken aback by the vitriol. Anonymity almost certainly plays a part here, as it does not take courage to be rude or slanderous if you cannot be held accountable for what you write. The lack of civility also derives from the growing reality that people do not live in proximity to or regularly interact with people who hold very different views on matters of politics, race, or religion. This "sorting" of our society in which we increasingly choose to live among people we find similar in ways that matter reinforces divisions and intolerance and leads to incivility.

One thing that comes to mind here is Washington, D.C. As recently as several decades ago elected officials spent much of their time in the nation's capital, bringing their families with them and going home only at intervals to campaign or see their constituents. They would see other members of Congress or executive branch officials or foreign diplomats or journalists in the course of their daily lives. Their children would attend the same schools. Today, by contrast, the average U.S. representative arrives in Washington on Tuesday morning and leaves late Thursday—and then only when Congress is in session. Their schedules tend to be packed. Families mostly stay behind in their home state or district. This lack of informal interaction contributes to the tribalism of our society and politics. There are precious few "neutral" spaces where those of differing parties and perspectives come together outside of the formal workplace.

I much enjoyed hearing tales of the friendship between two Supreme Court associate justices, Ruth Bader Ginsburg and Antonin Scalia. They went to the opera, shared dinner, even vacationed together. What makes this noteworthy is that the gap between the legal philosophies of the liberal Ginsburg and the conservative Scalia was so considerable. They disagreed frequently and fiercely, but were open about learning from one another. Ginsburg was quoted saying Scalia's dissents forced her to rewrite and, in the process, strengthen the rationale for her decisions; Scalia, for his part, when asked how he could be such good friends with someone he so often disagreed with, replied, "I attack ideas. I don't attack people." Their relationship was a model we would all do well to emulate.

Elsewhere in this book I suggest the utility of spending some time watching news shows or reading columnists or visiting websites with which you tend to disagree. It will help you better understand the thinking behind those who hold differing views; it might even lead you to reconsider your own views in whole or in part. A related idea is simply to spend some time over coffee or a meal with someone you know who holds very different political positions. The goal is not to persuade them to come over to yours but to come away with a better appreciation of one another's views and to build a foundation of respect and trust that allows both of you to spend time with one another despite your disagreements.

I also want to point out what civility is not. Civility does not mean pulling your punches or avoiding inconvenient facts or truths. Too much of what passes for public debate is marked by what is not said because it is politically incorrect or makes some uncomfortable. Public debate needs to make us uncomfortable if we are to understand the views of others and if the best assessments and recommendations for policy are to emerge. As preachers have been known to point out, speech is meant to afflict the comfortable, not just comfort the afflicted. The obligation here is to respect the right of free expression no matter how much we may disagree with what it is we hear or read.

Those who oversee opinion pages in newspapers or public assemblies in academic and other institutions would do well to remember this. Schools, colleges, and universities have a special responsibility to provide forums to those holding views across the political spectrum and to make sure speakers are allowed to speak. Codes of conduct for students, faculty, and staff need to stipulate what is permissible and the sanctions, such as suspension or expulsion, for those who violate them. Similarly, opinion pages of major newspapers that provide a space for independent editorials (op-eds) should include a wide range of perspectives. Where something offends some in the community the correct response is not to rescind an invitation or shout down a speech or refuse to publish an opinion piece but to offer an opportunity for rebuttal and debate and, ideally, learning. For now, though, the reality could hardly be more different.

In short, there is nothing civil about trying to silence those with whom you disagree, especially when it involves denying someone a venue (and the opportunity to write or speak) they deserve to have. Illiberalism is unacceptable be it of the political left or right. Here again, the right of free speech must take priority. What civility is not about is censorship.

OBLIGATION V

Reject Violence

One characteristic that makes a government sovereign is that it holds a monopoly on the legitimate use of force within its borders. The one exception to this is self-defense, as any individual has that right under the law and common sense. I say this recognizing that what constitutes self-defense is anything but clear-cut and varies from state to state and jury to jury.

When individuals or groups turn to violence, be it to enrich themselves or settle a personal score or for some other reason, it is considered a crime. Here I would list organized crime and those who rob banks, commit rape, carry out murder, and obviously much else. The use of armed force against civilians or authorities by individuals and groups for political purposes, however, is something entirely different and has another name: terrorism. It is a direct threat to public order—a prerequisite for all that consti-tutes normal activity in a society—and can interrupt everything from business and education to politics and travel.

What makes a democracy different from authoritarian sys-tems is that democracy offers peaceful channels for individuals and groups to pursue their political and economic policy aims. They do so without any guarantee that they will achieve their goals, but they accept the legitimacy of the process, as they be-lieve they will have a fair chance of succeeding in part or in whole over time. They also believe that no particular issue merits under-mining the value of the political system as a whole.

Nevertheless, the temptation arises from time to time for some to pursue political goals with physical force. It can stem from conviction, that a goal is so worthy that the ends justify the means, or from frustration, that there is no other available path to take to achieve one's goals and that the goals are judged to be so important they must be met no matter the price.

There are, however, significant problems with resorting to physical violence in the pursuit of political goals. There is the like-lihood of casualties among people who have done nothing other than disagree with those acting violently or, in the case of police, simply doing their job by protecting people and promoting order. There is also the chance that those who simply find themselves in the wrong place at the wrong time will become collateral damage and end up injured or worse.

Regular, widespread uses of force that cannot be turned back by rightful authorities threaten democracy and even the country. If organized between two factions, for example, such violence can lead to civil war, something the United States has experienced but once in its two and a half centuries. Less organized but still widespread uses of force become indistinguishable from anarchy, which leaves every citizen vulnerable and creates circumstances in which many citizens would give up democracy in exchange for a repressive political system that promises to offer them protection and maintain civil peace.

Even short of such extremes there is the risk that political issues will get lost amid violence. Instead, the conversation tends to become one about means rather than ends. It can be counterproductive, as violence will alienate many who might otherwise agree in part or in whole with the articulated ends but reject the means. And as just noted, violence can invite a response in kind, such that those with competing goals will likewise turn to violence. Vigilantism could well develop. If the scale of the violence grows, it can threaten public order and the ability of all that constitutes what we take for granted as normal life to go on. It is hard to imagine a context less suited for promoting debate and compromise.

Should the use of force also prove "successful," it sets a terrible precedent that others will likely try to emulate to achieve their goals. It increases the odds that sooner or later those who oppose the side that emerged through violence will turn to violence to overthrow or replace it. Moreover, gaining power through violence robs those involved of any legitimacy. They will be able to govern only through coercion and by shutting down the normal mechanisms for dissent and shared decision-making. Democracy by definition will have disappeared.

There are multiple alternatives to using violence in pursuit of political ends. One is to double down on efforts to bring about desired policy change within the law and within the system. This can be done through greater effort, be it by registering more citizens to vote or getting more registered voters out to the polls to cast their votes. It can also be sought by supporting policy change through legislation or executive action at the local, state, or national level. Constitutional amendment is an additional path.

There is as well another tack: civil disobedience, or nonviolent political action that contravenes the law. The term "civil disobedience" can be traced back to Henry David Thoreau, a mid-nineteenth century New England thinker who refused to pay taxes as a protest against slavery and the war with Mexico. Thoreau was prepared to go to prison for his stance and did. It turns out this willingness to accept the penalties imposed by existing authority is central to the concept. Civil disobedience as developed by Thoreau constitutes an action within the existing system, not a rejection of it or an attempt to replace or overthrow it.

Protest, in the sense of organizing rallies critical of existing legal and political arrangements seen as unjust, immoral, or misguided, can be a more active form of civil disobedience. Like

Thoreau's refusal to pay taxes, protest is not necessarily a revolutionary action, as it takes place within the existing order and seeks to change it. Such protest is what former civil rights leader and congressman John Lewis termed "good trouble, necessary trouble." A protester acting within the order is prepared to pay a price (be it a fine or imprisonment) for their behavior—and they carry out their protest or actions peacefully.

Among the leading practitioners of nonviolent protest in history were Mahatma Gandhi and Martin Luther King Jr. Gandhi was a lawyer who more than anyone else developed the thinking and practices associated with nonviolent resistance in pursuit of political aims. For Gandhi, the aim was to bring about Indian independence from Britain. Gandhi employed marches, rallies, strikes, negotiations, and boycotts. He endured multiple arrests but never resorted to violence, believing correctly that occupying the political high ground would keep the focus on the immorality and costs of British policy rather than that of the Indians seeking independence. He also thought he could win over a substantial slice of public opinion in Great Britain if he acted with restraint on behalf of his cause. By 1947, helped in no small part by British exhaustion stemming from World War II, Gandhi achieved his goal.

Martin Luther King Jr. was trained as a minister and became one of the leaders of the American Civil Rights Movement. He too espoused nonviolence and opted instead for marches, rallies, speeches, boycotts, and acts of defiance, for example taking a seat in the front of a bus when Black people were required to sit in the rear or demanding food service at a lunch counter reserved for Whites only. Like Gandhi, he appealed to the conscience and pocketbook of the nation. His goal was not revolution but rather reform. In the end, he proved largely successful, as many of the barriers based on race were taken down and made illegal by a series of laws passed in the 1960s that protected the rights of all Americans regardless of color.

What both of these movements had in common was that they sought to win over relevant public opinion by shining a light on existing practices that were fundamentally discriminatory and unfair. Violence was mostly avoided as it would have meant forfeiting the high ground and having the message lost amid the mayhem. It was also anything but clear that violence would have achieved the desired end.

I want to make clear that I am not suggesting that civil disobedience and nonviolence are always the best route to desirable political change. Indeed, they require a context in which authorities are prepared to act with restraint when it comes to ordering police and military units to use force against protesters. Civil disobedience also has a much better chance of advancing political aims if there is an active, free press and social media ready to shine a spotlight on conditions that gave rise to the protest, spread the word among protesters, and call out any abuses of power by state authorities. The two successful historical cases cited above— colonial India against Great Britain and the American Civil Rights Movement—all succeeded in no small part because of what the government was unwilling to do when it came to crushing dissent. It is far from evident that such tactics would succeed in reforming authoritarian or dictatorial political systems in countries such as North Korea, Russia, China, or most countries of the Middle East that are willing and able to do whatever is required, no matter the toll in lives, to maintain control and power. But one of the things that makes democracies unique is their openness to challenge and their capacity for change. The change may not be sufficiently fast or dramatic for some, but some change now with the potential for more later is infinitely preferable to anarchy or civil conflict.

Much of this discussion has concerned itself with those advocating for change. But there are as well obligations for those who hold power and exert influence. It goes beyond the necessary condemnation of any who resort to violence for political ends and willingness to see that those involved pay the required legal price. What happened in Washington on January 6, 2021, for example, cannot be allowed to be swept under the rug. The notion, as the Republican National Committee put forward in a statement on February 4, 2022, that what took place constituted "legitimate political discourse" is preposterous; infinitely closer to the truth was the characterization of Mitch McConnell, the Republican leader in the Senate: "It was a violent insurrection for the purpose of trying to prevent the peaceful transfer of power after a legitimately certified election." Such politically inspired violence meets the definition of terrorism. Those who incite political violence should also be held accountable; free speech is protected but is not an absolute. The Supreme Court has ruled that those calling for "imminent lawless action" are little or no different from those who carry out the violence and are liable. The problem with the imminence threshold, however (and the associated point that what is said must be shown as "likely to incite or produce such action"), is that it is virtually impossible to prove it has been met. Courts lean in favor of protecting free speech even when it tips over into encouraging dangerous, irresponsible actions. One could fairly argue that regardless of this legal threshold those with power and influence should not be advocating for political violence in any situation. If because of the fine points of the law those who advocate for violence do so in a form that allows them to escape legal and civil penalties, they should still pay a political price. That is something only citizens can bring about.

But responsibility does not end there. The need to minimize political violence also requires that a premium be placed on making the political and legal system fair and responsive, that there be a level playing field. This holds especially true for those entrusted with special power, such as the police. Acceptance of the legitimacy of the state and its monopoly on the use of force is predicated on its willingness to exercise restraint, to use force lawfully, and to hold anyone who is an officer of the state accountable. This is necessary to reduce the chance that American democracy will fall victim to widespread violence.

OBLIGATION VI

Value Norms

The necessity of obeying the law is obvious. It is not just the penalties, from fines to imprisonment, that potentially follow if we do not, but also the recognition that no society of any sort, much less a democratic one, can endure amid widespread lawlessness. Order is a necessary prerequisite for everything we value, from the personal to the professional and from the mundane to the profound.

Norms, though, are something else—and something more. Norms are the unwritten traditions, rules, customs, conventions, codes of conduct, and practices that reduce friction and brittleness in a society. Words like "cushion" and "lubricant" come to mind. Laws provide the scaffolding of a society, but norms are what fill it in and make it livable, the furniture within the building, so to speak.

The argument here is that observance of the law and, to be more precise, the letter of the law is necessary but insufficient for this or any democracy to endure much less thrive. Observance of norms is required as well. Norms are related to the spirit and intent of the law, to behaviors that for one reason or another cannot be legislated or formally required but that all the same are desirable, even essential, for a democracy to be successful.

This matters because it is impossible to reduce every potential behavior of consequence to something as specific and fixed as law. It is simply impossible to anticipate every situation and to make it a matter of law. In many cases there is also the reality that what is undesirable may not constitute something that should or can be made illegal. But no less true is that certain behaviors should be discouraged and others encouraged if the society and democracy are to do well.

Norms play an important role in our own lives. Some constitute obligations that make up this book. To remain civil. To look out for one's neighbors and fellow citizens. Other norms that influence our lives are more personal. To give a portion of our income or wealth to charity, to help those less fortunate. To respect authority. To demonstrate good sportsmanship. To tell the truth. To keep our commitments.

Most of the norms discussed here are more political, meant to be observed by elected and appointed officials. Ideally, they will do so. But we know from experience that many will not; as one astute observer who immigrated here from a country whose democracy was undone from within noted, "Norms are unspoken and ill defined, making them vulnerable." This is precisely why people must hold political figures to account when they violate norms.

Perhaps the most basic norm of American democracy is the tradition of accepting election results. Acceptance of electoral outcomes should be linked to process, not results. Those who are eligible to vote should not be obstructed from doing so and their votes must be accurately counted. The challenge is to make sure de facto barriers are not erected to make voting difficult for some groups, say, by the party holding decisive power limiting the number of polling stations or when they are open in certain districts known to tilt toward the other party.

Fraud, be it stuffing ballot boxes, not counting votes, or allowing ineligible voters to vote, is extremely rare in the United States, and does not exist on a scale that affects outcomes. The result is that the tradition has grown up of accepting election results except in the small percentage of instances in which the vote is so close that a recount is required by law or warranted. There is nothing in the Constitution about concession speeches or congratulatory phone calls from the defeated candidate to the victor. There is no requirement that an outgoing president ride up Pennsylvania Avenue with his successor and attend his or her swearing in. But with few exceptions this is just what has taken place. This is the norm.

This acceptance of elections is critical. It is essential that those who did not support the winning candidate see the person who goes on to govern as legitimate, as the rightful holder of the office that was contested. Their ability to do their job depends on it. Authority seen as illegitimate will not have its decisions accepted and implemented; nor will it be seen as a partner for governing. Rejection of election outcomes also becomes a context in which politically motivated violence becomes more frequent and serious.

In 2000, Democratic candidate and incumbent vice president Al Gore did not question the accuracy or legitimacy of the result despite a strong case for doing so based on the controversial vote count in Florida. Gore specifically explained his concession and acceptance of the disputed count as something he decided to do "for the sake of our unity as a people and the strength of our democracy." Richard Nixon also receives rare credit from a number of historians for rejecting the counsel of advisers urging him to challenge the outcome of the close 1960 presidential election even though there were credible reports of voter fraud, reportedly telling those advisers that "it'd tear the country to pieces. You can't do that."

The norm at work here is not simply the acceptance of electoral defeat; in principle, there would be nothing wrong in rejecting an outcome that had been fundamentally altered because of improper voting or vote counting. But there would need to be strong evidence this was the case and then it would need to be pursued through established legal channels. To claim that fraud has occurred in the absence of evidence—as has been done in the aftermath of the 2020 presidential election by former President Donald Trump and many of his supporters in the Congress and beyond—or to charge fraud before votes are cast and counted—as was done by the leading Republican candidate for governor in the 2021 recall referendum in California—is something fundamentally different.

Observance of a number of other norms is similarly essential if democracy is to fare well. Elected and senior appointed officials should accept the independent role of the media. This translates into making themselves available to the media on a regular basis. Legitimate journalists—as opposed to political activists masquerading as journalists—ought to be treated with respect. To describe journalists as "the enemy of the people," as President Trump did on multiple occasions, violates the norm that accepts a free press as essential in a democracy, even if at times what media outlets print is problematic politically or inaccurate. In a representative democracy, the media is in a unique position to shine a light on those with power and how they wield it. Without a free press we likely would not have learned about the crimes of Watergate or the flawed decision-making central to the Vietnam War. As Thomas Jefferson famously put it, "Were it left to me to decide whether we should have a government without newspapers or newspapers without a government, I should not hesitate a moment to prefer the latter." Answers to questions posed by the media can provide understanding of what those with power are planning and doing and why. Our ability to be informed citizens in no small part depends on this.

Another norm involves the release of tax returns on the part of candidates for high office. Yes, this raises questions about privacy, but the argument can be made that this is part of what is expected of people who choose to run. If we are going to grant someone political power, we should know that there are no conflicts of interest and that the individual is pursuing the public good. Details as to charitable contributions can tell us something about character and social conscience. So too can the use of what might be described as aggressive tax-avoiding loopholes.

Appointing only those who are qualified to positions of responsibility is a norm, one that is often violated when politicians appoint their relatives. Allowing legal processes to play out without political pressure is yet another. Recusing or removing oneself from participating in decisions in which a close relative is involved (something judges including Supreme Court justices are expected to do) qualifies. Telling the truth is a particularly important norm if citizens are not to grow alienated from their government and political process. Except in rare instances when testifying under oath before Congress or a jury, there is no legal requirement for public officials—or the rest of us for that matter—to tell the truth. Yet confidence and faith in government depends on doing so, as does our collective ability to hold debates over policy. As noted earlier, serious debate must rest on a foundation of facts, and statements and actions that blur the truth are corrosive.

Not revealing to unauthorized persons the content of certain deliberations or written material—not leaking—also deserves singling out. This is a legal requirement when it comes to information classified (protected) on national security grounds. But the obligation exists more broadly when divulging what is being considered would undermine the integrity of the decision-making process. Privacy is often required for there to be an honest, comprehensive assessment of developments and policies, and partial or premature exposure of what is being said or considered can make it impossible for there to be a fair or rigorous assessment of all options. Leaking invariably undermines trust, leading to a narrowing of those involved in decision-making and a reticence by participants to write or say anything controversial, all of which tends to lead to poorer policy outcomes.

To be sure, there is always the option of trying to codify norms into rules or laws. More than anything else, such an action takes certain behaviors or decisions out of the hands of individuals and removes the opportunity for them to act legally but inappropriately or unwisely. This was done, for example, after the presidency of Franklin Delano Roosevelt. FDR was the first and last president to serve more than two four-year terms. The moment was extraordinary because of the Great Depression and World War II, and Roosevelt was an extraordinary individual and president, but as a rule extraordinary situations make for bad precedents. In this case, the fear was and is that anyone serving too long as president could accumulate too much power. The result was the Twenty-second Amendment, ratified in 1951, that limited a president to one election and one reelection (or to ten years if he or she ascended to the presidency because of the removal or death of the president). The terms need not be consecutive for this limitation to apply.

Another norm—that appointed civil service employees in the executive branch ought to be kept separate from political activities in the conduct of their job—was made law in 1939. The so-called Hatch Act bans civil servants from performing political tasks—for instance, cabinet members participating in campaign rallies—at the same time that it protects them from being coerced into performing such tasks or paying a penalty (including losing their job) for refusing to do so. A related norm is not to use the powers of government for partisan purposes—for example, by ordering unwarranted tax audits or legal investigations into one's political opponents.

More recently, and in still another realm, there have been efforts to prohibit senators and representatives from buying and selling shares of stock in individual corporations. The reason is that they have access to privileged information that could give them an advantage when it comes to decisions affecting the purchase or sale of stocks. Ideally, individuals who are in such a position would observe the norm of not taking advantage of their position, but as we have seen in recent years, not all can be counted on to do so. Absent such a ban, it is up to the media to ask questions and voters to penalize those politicians who exploit their position for personal gain. Codifying this norm, though, so that representatives cannot buy or sell stocks while in office, could prove an even better remedy.

That said, there will be limits to what can be written into law. As noted earlier, it is impossible to imagine every behavior judged undesirable. Or there may be disagreement over just how undesirable it is and as a result insufficient political support to codify some prohibition. Or there may be grounds for not instituting a ban lest special circumstances arise. All of which helps reinforce why norms can be both desirable and necessary. We like to think of ourselves as a nation of laws, but the truth is that democracy requires more than laws if it is to function. Only the observation of norms can do this, and it will happen only if citizens insist on it.

OBLIGATION VII

Promote the Common Good

We all live in a context, in a society. We have a stake in the overall well-being of that society, which in turn translates into our having a stake in the well-being of our fellow citizens. As poet and priest John Donne wrote, "No man is an island entire of itself; every man is a piece of the continent, a part of the main."

There are both moral and practical reasons for caring about our fellow Americans. The former is simply caring for others for their sake. The question is a familiar one: Am I my brother's or sister's keeper? To some extent we should be and need to be. This teaching can be found in many of the world's major religions. The New Testament instructs, "Look not every man on his own things, but every man also on the things of others." In Judaism, the notion is captured by the theme that "all of Israel are responsible for one other." Various Hindu texts contain verses that elaborate on the theme of the world as one family, calling on individuals to treat others equally and as they would want to be treated. This sense of obligation to one's fellow man or woman is the basis of a great deal of volunteerism and charity. At best this is an argument for choosing to do good things that assist others; at a minimum, it is an argument for avoiding doing things that injure others.

There is another reason for caring about others. Doing so reflects our self-interest and is for our own sake. Martin Luther King Jr. made such an argument in his "Letter from a Birmingham Jail": "We are caught in an inescapable network of mutuality, tied in a single garment of destiny. Whatever affects one directly affects all indirectly." In many ways the trajectories of other people's lives intersect with our own and the consequences can be significant and, unfortunately, not always beneficial. Strangers and neighbors alike can be sources of contagion by carrying infectious disease or a burden on public health stemming from abuse of drugs or alcohol. People can turn to crime for a host of reasons and even if there is no intent can act irresponsibly with guns or cars. Then there is the reality that there are those who do not contribute what they could to society and the economy and as a result increase the financial burden of the rest of us. All this adds up to a strong case that the obligation to care for others, be it for their sake or our own, is critical for a democratic society. Teddy Roosevelt, in his inaugural address more than a century ago, posited that "our relations with the other powers of the world are important, but still more important are our relations among ourselves."

What makes it all complicated is that sooner or later the matter of one's obligations to fellow citizens can come into tension with individual rights.

Before looking at specific instances, it is helpful to refer back to the writings of John Stuart Mill, the nineteenth-century British philosopher, who tackled this very issue. In his 1859 treatise *On Liberty*, Mill articulated what has become known as the Harm Principle, which argues that individuals should be free to do what they want, even if it causes harm to themselves, but not if it causes harm to others. The Harvard legal philosopher Zechariah Chafee quoted an anonymous judge when he wrote in 1919 that "your right to swing your arms ends where the other man's nose begins."

Explicit in Mill's writing is that government should not interfere in individual actions except when others suffer harm as a result. Mill's logic would exempt legal restrictions or penalties linked to sex practices between consenting adults or, for that matter, suicide. It is related to what we think of as libertarianism but with the caveat that maximizing individual autonomy and minimizing government intervention should not come at the expense of collective welfare.

Take smoking. In principle we should all have the right to smoke if we want to, despite the overwhelming evidence that smoking can kill the smoker. Judged from the standard set by

Mill, smoking appears to be acceptable, something dangerous but not worthy of government restrictions except in the case of minors, since they are presumably not yet in a position to make responsible choices for themselves.

But the calculation quickly gets more complex. When smokers become ill, this is a burden on the health-care system and the society more generally, as it leads to early exit from the work force. So we all indirectly subsidize those who smoke by paying higher health-care premiums or disability payments or by not benefitting from what they might contribute to the economy and to the government via taxes. It is not at all clear, though, whether such harm would be sufficiently great to justify government intervention.

Most relevant is that smoking poses a direct health threat to others. Those who breathe in secondhand smoke can become ill even if they themselves are not smoking. This is what led to limits or bans of smoking in public places and shared spaces, from bars and restaurants to trains, buses, planes, and offices. Quite simply, my right to health, to clean air, and to not breathe in your smoke outweighs your right to smoke. Again, returning to Mill, smoking is fair game for government intervention and regulation, as it can harm others.

Much the same holds when it comes to safe driving. We accept speed limits and observe traffic lights when we drive, even though they represent an infringement on our ability to drive at whatever speed we choose. Such limits protect us from ourselves, and, more important, protect others lest we drive so fast we lose control and injure them. You could argue the same when it comes to drinking or texting while driving; the right to enjoy alcohol or to look at email does not offset our obligation not to endanger others.

There is one more layer of complexity to consider. The government also mandates the use of seat belts even though no one else is harmed if the driver or passenger elects not to wear them and suffers injury from an accident. The same holds true for motorcycle helmets, required to be worn in many states. Motivating the government to require seat belts and helmets is the belief that ensuring intelligent behavior sometimes justifies such intervention, to quite literally save people from themselves. (Seat belts, by the way, save some fifteen thousand lives a year and have saved an estimated four hundred thousand lives over the past fifty years.) What is noteworthy is that in these instances—as well as when it comes to limits on the availability and use of certain drugs—the reach of the "nanny state" is widely accepted even though it compromises the individual's choice or right not to take protective measures.

These and related arguments have come to the fore recently with the COVID-19 pandemic and resulting mask and vaccine mandates. Many Americans reject these mandates as an unacceptable infringement on their freedom to choose, in some cases giving up their jobs or access to schools or sporting events as a consequence.

This is not the first time government requirements for vaccination have been met with resistance. At the beginning of the previous century, the disease in question was smallpox. The Cambridge, MA, board of health issued an ordinance requiring that everyone get vaccinated or face a fine. Henning Jacobson, a local minister, refused, saying he and his son had suffered bad reactions to previous vaccinations and wanted no part of this one. What is more, he refused to pay the $5 fine. The case went all the way to the Supreme Court, which ruled that "the liberty secured by the Constitution of the United States does not import an absolute right in each person to be at all times, and in all circumstances wholly freed from restraint, nor is it an element in such liberty that one person, or a minority of persons residing in any community and enjoying the benefits of its local government, should have power to dominate the majority when supported in their action by the authority of the State. It is within the police power of a State to enact a compulsory vaccination law, and it is for the legislature, and not for the courts, to determine in the first instance whether vaccination is or is not the best mode for the prevention of smallpox and the protection of the public health."

Justice John Marshall Harlan's reasoning is worth presenting: "There is, of course, a sphere within which the individual may assert the supremacy of his own will and rightfully dispute the authority of any human government, especially of any free government existing under a written constitution. But it is equally true that in every well-ordered society charged with the duty of conserving the safety of its members the rights of the individual in respect of his liberty may at times, under the pressure of great dangers, be subjected to such restraint, to be enforced by reasonable regulations, as the safety of the general public may demand." Mill would both understand and agree.

Masks, as everyone knows, can be an uncomfortable inconvenience. They also happen to serve a dual purpose: they protect the wearer from airborne diseases spread by others and protect others in turn from diseases the wearer might spread. Vaccines likewise protect the vaccinated from the disease or dramatically reduce the severity of the illness if infection happens all the same. In addition, vaccines reduce the chance someone will be a carrier who in turn can infect others.

It is baffling that opposition to the COVID-19 vaccine should be as strong as it is given the vaccine's demonstrated effectiveness, its pristine safety record, and the obvious risks associated with contracting COVID-19. (As of this writing more than one million Americans and fifteen to twenty million people worldwide have lost their lives to COVID-19.) It is also curious in the sense that mandates for various vaccines, including smallpox, polio, measles, mumps, and chicken pox, were widely accepted for decades.

So why now? In many ways the answers can be found in other chapters of this book: in the spread of misinformation via social media and, at times, legacy media alike; in the reality that more of us live and work and socialize only with like-minded persons;

growing hostility toward and lack of familiarity with government; an increasingly widespread rejection of facts and the experts presenting them; and a declining respect for norms that have long guided individual behavior, a reduced propensity to compromise, and a near exclusive emphasis on rights when people consider their relationship with society and country. Rugged individualism, which is something often celebrated, is clearly on the upswing in this country. The problem is that it can all too easily descend into selfishness. Somehow opposition to masks and the COVID-19 vaccine have gotten caught up in the culture wars and become politicized. This is costly in many ways: hundreds of thousands of Americans have unnecessarily and avoidably lost their lives, school has been interrupted for many students and invaluable time lost, the economy has grown at a slower rate, lives have been put on hold and at risk. Again, what it underscores is what can happen if we fail to balance individual rights with obligations and our personal freedom with the public good. In such situations, everyone loses.

Let me introduce one other theme into this discussion of the obligation to commit to the common or public good. It is the importance of fairness, to ensure that the opportunity to realize the American dream, to get ahead, is available to all.

It turns out that equality of opportunity—in reality as well as on paper—is critical for the functioning of a democracy. At a minimum, fairness requires both the avoidance of discrimination that blocks equal opportunity and the provision of resources that make opportunity equal in practice as well as principle. The United States, or more specifically its economy and society, can reach its potential only if talent is developed and allowed to flourish. Talent can then be tapped for invention, innovation, resources, and skilled labor. All this benefits the individual directly as well as their family, community, and country.

By contrast, if Americans are denied equal opportunity, their potential contributions will be forfeited, and rather than adding ballast to the society and economy they could become a burden. What is more, if people are denied opportunities within the system, some will be tempted or motivated to go outside the system and press for their goals in a manner that is incompatible with democracy and many of the obligations advocated for in these pages, including nonviolence.

Equal opportunity is not to be equated or confused with equal outcomes. To the contrary, unequal outcomes in society are inevitable, the result of what we are born with, and what is garnered from effort, experience, opportunity, luck, and more. A society does, however, have to grapple with whether to limit inequality, either by forming a government-provided safety net or setting a ceiling on income, inheritance, or wealth through taxation, or some combination of the two.

Discrimination that limits the potential or options of individuals must be discouraged as much as possible when it cannot be explicitly prevented by law. Fairness also requires that what might be described as the circumstances of birth are not dispositive for those born without means. What and how much to provide in the way of a social floor, to whom, and how it is paid for are necessary and legitimate matters for political debate. This involves federal, state, and local government efforts (sometimes abetted by religious organizations, charities, corporations, and individuals). Included in this basket are programs that promote maternal and newborn health, early childhood and prekindergarten education and childcare, and much-improved public schools. It also includes making available scholarships to parochial, private, and charter schools as well as to community and four-year colleges and universities. Education, the social ladder described by Horace Mann in 1848 as "a great equalizer of the conditions of men," remains critical to the effort of making the American dream a reality.

It is for the courts and politics to decide whether—and, if so, how—past discrimination on matters of race, gender, and class ought to be factored into decision-making. In 2003, the Supreme Court ruled that race could be taken into account to improve the admissions prospects of underrepresented groups (and that doing so would not violate the Fourteenth Amendment's equal protection clause) so long as other factors also received consideration. Many believe race and gender should be taken into account in admissions, hiring, and promotion decisions but quotas, i.e., a specific number or level of assured outcomes, should be avoided.

Another approach is to instead focus on the long term, working to increase the presence of underrepresented groups in the pool or pipeline of people being trained for opportunities so that they can effectively and fairly compete with those who have had access to such opportunities earlier in their careers. It is also important to recognize that considering class might be as important, or even more so, than race and gender when it comes to ensuring that opportunity is equal throughout society.

No less controversial are steps that would limit the ability of schools, colleges, and universities to give preference to the children of wealthy parents or to those of alumni (what are often referred to as legacy or institutional admissions). Also hotly debated are efforts by the federal government or states to place a ceiling on what can be inherited or passed on to future generations tax free. The rationale is to level the playing field somewhat, to limit the advantages of some lest living in the United States become a race in which certain individuals enjoy an enormous head start. I would also argue that massive intergenerational transfers of wealth do not always end up helping the recipients as they can destroy the incentive to work hard. That said, I know many disagree with me here and believe there should be no "death taxes" or at least generous limits on what can be passed on to future generations with little or no tax. This too is an issue best resolved by the political process.

The emphasis should be on opportunity and making sure it is real in practice as well as in principle. This means preventing discrimination, increasing education and training so more Americans can hold their own in a competitive environment, and restricting advantages stemming from family wealth. If this is done, more equal outcomes will follow, and more Americans will experience the rewards of upward mobility. Just as important, it should be done in a manner that minimizes grievances and the sense that the gains of some have come at the expense of others. Fairness is a concept that is central to the smooth and peaceful functioning of a society, and whatever is done to make the American dream a reality and promote the common good must be done with this in mind.

OBLIGATION VIII

Respect Government Service

There is a strong American tradition of suspicion toward government. This book began with the history of American democracy, and even though the Constitution was drafted and ratified to replace the ineffective Articles of Confederation, the flaws of the Articles did not prevent many from having doubts about the wisdom of replacing it with a much stronger government. The fear was that the successor government would constrain the rights of both states and individuals. The result was the Bill of Rights, which articulated the rights of individuals and states and provided an architecture that limited the sway of the federal government and the executive branch in particular.

Over the centuries, this fear of too powerful a government has morphed into something of a dislike of government full stop. Ronald Reagan used this as part of his stump speech, exclaiming that "the nine most terrifying words in the English language are: 'I'm from the government, and I'm here to help.'" And even more cynically: "Government's view of the economy could be summed up in a few short phrases: If it moves, tax it. If it keeps moving, regulate it. And if it stops moving, subsidize it."

Much of what Reagan had to say supported his aim to reduce taxation and, on occasion, spending; it was also often said with a wink, as Reagan clearly understood this was red meat for his political base. In recent years, though, we have seen frequent reference to the "deep state," which is a much darker idea suggesting that within the government there are careerists who are loyal only to themselves and who seek to take away freedom from Americans they disagree with. If this sounds like the stuff of conspiracy, it is because it is. What began as opposition to strong government and big government has morphed into outright hostility of government and rejection of its legitimacy and authority. Not surprisingly, polls indicate that public trust in government is near historic lows (only around one in four Americans express trust), although the number varies when one asks about particular government functions and when the vote is broken down by party. Both Democrats and Republicans are more trusting of government when one of their own occupies the White House.

Don't get me wrong. Governments make mistakes, sometimes big ones, with enormous consequences. Power does get abused. Citizens are at times lied to. Money is wasted. Corruption exists. Racism is tolerated or even advanced. The wealthy often enjoy a degree of power, influence, and access that ordinary citizens do not. Wars of choice are launched that cost lives and money in pursuit of aims that are anything but vital.

The good news, though, is that American democracy has the tools to deal with such behavior. The free press can report on poor decision-making and execution and uncover corruption. Congress can hold hearings and place a spotlight on government action and curtail military interventions as it did in Vietnam. Whistleblowers can call attention to abuses of power. Law enforcement can intervene to investigate criminality. The court system can and does provide fair trials and intercede in contested elections. In extreme cases, remedies such as impeachment are available. History demonstrates the capacity for uncovering mistakes, introducing reform, and voting out of power those who have failed to use it well or honestly.

Given how important government is, the reaction to imperfect or flawed government performance should be better government. Think about it. Government provides for our physical security against criminals, terrorists, and foreign militaries; designs and carries out our foreign policy; builds the roads, airports, bridges, rails, and tunnels that make up the country's infrastructure; makes sure the water we drink, food we eat, and air we breathe is safe; sets aside resources for retirees, children, the disabled, and the unemployed; operates public schools and hospitals and sets standards for private institutions; licenses those with a large impact on their fellow citizens, including doctors, lawyers, teachers, and engineers; makes sure the currency is valued and accepted; protects individuals and groups against discrimination; sets a minimum wage; oversees an economy that is the world's largest in a manner meant to limit inflation; creates jobs; encourages entrepreneurs; and provides a floor for the less fortunate.

All this is done by people—nearly 25 million of them. Some 9 million Americans work in or for the federal government, including 1.4 million active-duty military, and far more work for state or local governments. They make decisions affecting the allocation of something on the order of $6 trillion a year, roughly one-third the entire U.S. economy. The deep state is us.

We should therefore want the best and brightest among us to work in government, be it for a time or for a career. To be clear, the overwhelming percentage of those who work in the federal branch are civil servants. A president gets to appoint on the order of four thousand people to senior positions. Whether someone is a political appointee or a civil servant, there are limits to how we can compensate those in government; there is no way this compensation can compete with Wall Street or Fortune 500 companies. What we can do is offer these people our respect. We also want them to exercise their best judgment, which includes pushing back against those elected representatives and political appointees whose agendas are questionable or illegal. We need to protect and reward those who do so, both whistleblowers and those who speak truth to power even when those with power are in no mood to hear it. The structure of American government is designed to emphasize transparency and distribution of power. This argues for making sure the civil service is strong enough to challenge political authority while we root out those civil servants who are incompetent or corrupt or are pursuing political agendas of their own. This is something very different than a proposal reportedly under consideration by some Republicans that would grant a president wide discretion in firing career civil servants.

Modifying how we see and talk about those who work in government would help. But it is not enough. We also need to consider making government service far more common than it is. Right now, working for the government is entirely voluntary; there has not been a military draft for nearly fifty years. The military would not benefit from a draft that provided short-term involvement of many who did not want to be there. What is more, the all-volunteer force is a success and should not be fixed, as it is not broken. And as valuable as universal government or national service might be, attempting to mandate it would likely be counterproductive as it would stimulate significant pushback from many across the political spectrum who would see it as government overreach.

Incentivizing government service, though, would be altogether different. Why should we want young Americans to perform one or two years of government service? One reason is that a common experience would help break down some of the barriers that have arisen owing to geography, class, race, religion, education, language, and more. World War II did precisely this for millions of Americans. Today, however, there is simply too little common experience in this society and too much that reinforces differences and divisions. It is revealing that according to a recent poll, almost half of second-year college students report they wouldn't choose to room with someone who supported a different presidential candidate than they did in 2020, while a majority say they wouldn't go on a date with someone who voted differently and nearly two-thirds couldn't envision marrying someone who supported a different candidate. As a result, trust—essential if people in a society are to work together constructively—is in short supply. An added benefit of more widespread national service is that it would also expose young people to government, breaking down the perception of government as alien from the people.

Options for government service could range from the military to civilian tasks that include teaching, building and maintaining infrastructure, community service, and overseas development. In addition, legislation has been introduced that would create a "Civilian Climate Corps" in which young Americans would undertake tasks ranging from forestation to bolstering resilience to climate change.

There have been government-created and supported programs in the past. FDR's Great Depression-inspired Civilian Conservation Corps (CCC) comes to mind. More recent examples include the Peace Corps, VISTA, Teach for America, Senior Corps, the National Civilian Community Corps, and others, many of which are grouped under AmeriCorps. Ideally, many young Americans would opt to work in some government capacity for one or two years. The opportunity, and the incentive to grasp it, could be enhanced by providing those who do so with access to grants or loans for education, along the lines of the G.I. Bill, or by forgiving some or all of an individual's student debt. Ideally, the one- or two-year experience would include training in basic work and life skills and civics education.

Practices elsewhere are instructive. Some sixty countries maintain active military conscription, which generally runs from one to three years. A handful require service for women as well as men. Nigeria has a "National Youth Service Corps" requiring a year of service in either military or civil programs. Young people are posted away from their hometowns in an effort to "promote national unity and integration." Several European countries are debating implementing or experimenting with voluntary service programs with civilian as well as military options. Israel, which requires between two and three years of military service for men and women at the age of eighteen, after high school graduation, provides a compelling case for national service. To be sure, there are meaningful exemptions from service in Israel, and these have only added to the large gap that has emerged between secular and religious Israelis, owing to the ability of the orthodox to avoid national service. But the otherwise shared experience has proved to be an invaluable tool to integrate immigrants, who learn Hebrew and skills. It brings together young Israelis who otherwise would likely never meet, much less have something in common. And those Israelis who go on to college after serving are more mature and experienced in the world.

Government service thus promises multiple payoffs. It would help to challenge the inaccurate and counterproductive perception that government is remote and unresponsive or, worse yet, an occupied foreign power. It is thus fully consistent with the obligation to get involved. The experience might just encourage some of our most talented young people to serve in the government or even to make it their career. If so, we would all benefit. And it would reduce some of the sorting that has caused too many Americans to not know, much less understand and respect, their fellow Americans. That would be a good return on investment by any measure.

OBLIGATION IX

Support the Teaching of Civics

This obligation draws inspiration from the Jewish festival of Passover. This annual holiday celebrates the liberation of the Jews some three thousand years ago from Pharaoh's Egypt, where they had been enslaved. Observed in the spring, the holiday is traditionally celebrated not in the synagogue but in the home, reflecting the fact that for much of their history Jews did not have access to the holy temple in Jerusalem. The service and dinner on the first and sometimes second nights of the holiday are one and the same. Activities are carried out in a specific sequence (the word for the meal—"seder"—is the Hebrew word for "order") and virtually everything done and eaten symbolizes something relevant to the narrative.

The script for the meal is provided by a book known as the Haggadah, literally translated from Hebrew as "the telling." It is derived from the biblical injunction in the book of Exodus that "thou shalt tell thy son (child) on that day, saying: It is because of that which the Lord did for me when I came forth out of Egypt." Motivating this requirement is the desire to make sure that every generation understands what it means to be a Jew, why it is of value, and what it requires. None of this is assumed. The telling of this history has proved to be invaluable, enabling the Jewish people to survive through the ages despite the fact they were few in number (even today there are only some fifteen million Jews in the world out of nearly eight billion people), frequently minorities without a homeland of their own, and often persecuted or killed for their beliefs.

The lesson is clear: No people should assume their history, their heritage, and what is central to it, is widely known among them much less automatically handed down. Collective identity, along with an appreciation and understanding of what lies behind it, is a matter of teaching, not biology. This is true of particular groups of people, be they defined by religion or gender or race or geography or history. It is no less true of a people who constitute a nation, in this case the American nation.

What worries me and what in no small part gave rise to this book is that we are failing to fulfill the obligation to pass down the essentials of what it means to be an American and citizen of the United States of America. Ironically, this does not apply to the newest citizens, immigrants. They often understand this country and its worth as much or more than anyone. After all, they chose to come here. They studied to pass the exam required for citizenship. They often escaped a country where economic opportunities were limited, where they did not have the freedom to speak their minds or practice their religions. In many cases, they voted with their feet so they could vote.

Instead, I am alluding to the many Americans who were born and grew up here but never received a proper understanding of their heritage or forgot what they once knew. It is instructive that Ronald Reagan devoted the traditional warning found in many presidential farewell addresses to just this point. He began by noting his satisfaction with the "resurgence of national pride," what he called the "new patriotism," that occasioned his presidency, but then added this: "This national feeling is good, but it won't count for much, and it won't last unless it's grounded in thoughtfulness and knowledge. An informed patriotism is what we want. And are we doing a good enough job teaching our children what America is and what she represents in the long history of the world?"

For Reagan, the answer to his question was an emphatic "No." How did this come to be? Many schools do not take it upon themselves to teach about this country, possibly because some assume the transmission of our past and its relevance for the present is automatic and already happening. Or they are not familiar with the central elements of the tradition. Or they do not value or agree with it. Or they have other priorities. Or they could not agree among themselves as to what needs to be taught.

The United States is particularly vulnerable to this failure to educate its citizens as to their heritage, as this is a country grounded not on a single religion or race or ethnicity (as are so many other countries) but on a set of ideas. These ideas are rooted in our history. Delineated in the Declaration of Independence, the new country made its case for breaking free from British rule as a necessary means to realizing the end of creating a society in which all men are created equal, endowed with certain unalienable rights, including life, liberty, and the pursuit of happiness. For its part, the government of the newly independent country would derive its mandate from the consent of the governed.

There are obviously major problems both with these words (the Declaration speaks of men, not people) and with the disconnect between the words and the American reality at the time, above all slavery, limits on rights for women, the treatment of the Indigenous peoples who were living here when the colonists arrived, and subsequent discrimination against multiple waves of immigrants. Nevertheless, the ideas represented a major step forward when they were articulated and remain relevant today. The notion that a person's fate is not determined by circumstances of birth over which he or she had no control is radical, as is the idea that government derives its legitimacy from those it governs, not from a hereditary family or a self-appointed few.

In a more perfect world, a book such as this would not be necessary because every American would get a grounding in civics—

in the country's political structures and traditions along with what is owed to and expected of its citizens—in elementary school, in high school, and, if they went on, in college. It would be reinforced by parents, family, and friends along with community, religious, corporate, labor, and political leaders. Journalists would likewise play a constructive role.

Alas, that is not the world we live in. There is a good deal of talk about the budget deficit. It may be that our civics deficit is of even greater consequence.

Only eight states and the District of Columbia require a full year of high school civics education. One state (Hawai'i) requires a year and a half, thirty-one states half a year, and ten states little or none. And if you are somehow reassured at all by these numbers, don't be, as the breadth and depth of what is taught is so uneven.

Things are little better at the next level. Less than a fifth of more than one thousand colleges and universities examined in one study require any civics education of students as a condition of graduation. The elite schools, including the Ivy League, are no better, and in fact tend to be worse, as many shy away from defining what it means to be educated. Unlike high schools, the problem is not that courses are not offered but rather that they are not required, and many students choose not to take what is available to them. Interestingly, the principal exception to this pattern is to be found in the service academies that educate future military leaders.

It should not surprise that surveys suggest that many Americans know and understand little about their own political system. Many do not value it highly. One-third believe violent action against the government is sometimes justified. These numbers suggest that the civics deficit will not turn into a balance much less a surplus if left to its own devices.

The question then is what to do about it. A basic idea is that no one should be able to graduate from a high school or college or university without a meaningful exposure to civics.

I write this in full knowledge that it is far easier to call for than to bring about. At the high school level, there is the problem of limited time and resources and requirements that other subjects be taught. It is essential to teach core intellectual skills—critical thinking along with the ability to perform basic math and learning to read as well as speak and write clearly—along with what are often described as noncognitive skills such as punctuality, perseverance, discipline, and the ability to work with others. Other subjects, be they science, physical education, language, and music and art, for good reason have powerful advocates and constituencies. Less so civics. There is the additional problem that few teachers are sufficiently trained to teach civics well. And on top of all this is the sheer scale and decentralization of American public schools: there are over thirteen thousand districts, 130,000 K-12 schools, three and a half million teachers, and tens of millions of students. Still, it is essential that public schools take on this task, as the one thing almost all Americans have to do is attend a school through the age of sixteen.

The problems at the country's approximately four thousand two- and four-year colleges and universities (attended for at least some time by about 60 percent of high school graduates) are different, in that most colleges and universities enjoy great discretion as to what they offer to students on campus and what they require of students before they can leave campus with a diploma under their arm. There are a handful of institutions that have a core curriculum with a significant number of required courses and a few at the opposite end of the spectrum that give students a free hand to determine what they study. But the most common approach is to have distribution requirements and to allow the individual student to choose among dozens of courses to fulfill each of those broad requirements in addition to what they need to do to satisfy what is called for in their major area of study.

The problem is that most students get through their college years with no exposure to civics, as studying it is not essential to graduate and can be easily avoided by choosing other courses to fulfill distribution requirements. The president of Johns Hopkins University in Baltimore could hardly be clearer about the result: "Our curricula have abdicated responsibility for teaching the habits of democracy."

Resistance comes from many directions. Professors tend to dislike teaching basic courses, preferring more specialized offerings reflecting their research. Students want to exert control over what they study; the priority for many, not surprisingly, is to take courses in those areas deemed practical and relevant in terms of future careers and compensation. There is also pressure on students to devote the bulk of their coursework to their major area of concentration, something that leaves only a limited amount of time for other pursuits. Administrations and boards of trustees for their part have failed to make the teaching of civics a priority and shy away from introducing core curricula lest they scare off students who do not want to be meaningfully constrained.

This could and should be fixed by simply introducing a required civics course for all students in high schools and universities. Such a commitment and mandate is likely to come about only from external pressure: from state governments that oversee high school funding and requirements, from parents who pay for education, from school administrations unafraid to define what they judge to be an adequate education (and differentiate themselves by doing so) even if it means some students will not apply, to those bodies that certify institutions of higher education. I would like to think requiring civics might actually become a selling point for those private and charter schools along with colleges and universities that do it. If some introduced the requirement and flourished, it could set in motion a truly healthy competition.

There is, though, what might be an even bigger problem: What to teach under the banner of civics? It is one thing to agree in principle that every student must study it and to make available the resources to teach it. But just what is "it"? Recent disputes over how to teach matters relating to race, which at times degenerated into violent confrontations, are an indication of how charged it can be to determine what children learn in schools. This is much more likely to be a problem in public high schools and publicly funded institutions of higher education, something that suggests experimentation might best begin in private and charter high schools and private colleges and universities and gradually cross over into the public realm once they are shown to be desirable.

A solid civics education would provide the basics as to the structure of government (the three federal branches, and state and local government, along with their scale and cost), how it operates (or is meant to operate) within and between the branches, and those terms and ideas fundamental to understanding American democracy, including democracy itself—representative versus direct democracy, republics, checks and balances, federalism, parties, impeachment, filibusters, gerrymandering, and so on. Both the rights and obligations of citizenship need highlighting. It should expose students to the basic texts of American democracy, including the Constitution, *The Federalist Papers*, pivotal Supreme Court decisions, major presidential speeches, and a handful of books that have stood the test of time. The curriculum should include the basics about American society and the American economy and how these facts have evolved over time. Teachers should emphasize the behaviors that democracy requires that parallel the obligations that constitute this book, i.e., the need for civility, the importance of compromise, the centrality of facts and where to find them.

Far more difficult is what to include in the way of history. There are any number of difficult questions: What events to include? What to emphasize? How to treat or cast certain historic phenomena or events? The "battle" between the 1619 and 1776 projects, two widely divergent narratives about the arc of American history, or subsequently over "critical race theory," highlights just how controversial and divisive history can be because of how it frames the past. My instinct here is to suggest that the major debates, events, and developments be studied, that any single framing be avoided, and where there is disagreement, that the various perspectives be presented. One possibility is for students to be assigned a range of readings and then asked to debate competing interpretations of the past. The "Where to Go for More" section at the end of this book also includes a list of resources that can provide a foundation for such inquiry.

As a rule of thumb, the curriculum should not try to settle contentious matters of history or the present or advocate for any particular policy so much as present facts, describe significant events, and set forth what were and are the major debates over analysis and policy prescriptions. Simulations, in which students participate in a model Congress or policy-making activity, could prove particularly useful. One could similarly imagine a mock press conference or Supreme Court hearing, or structured debates of every sort. Simulations offer an opportunity not just to encourage students to learn more about issues and institutions but also to put into practice democratic behaviors.

Over time, it would be ideal if something of a consensus emerged over what should be taught in the way of civics. Think about it: it seems borderline crazy that there would be competing approaches taught in different states or educational institutions if the goal is to build a common understanding of citizenship and the rights and obligations associated with it. But this is where we are, and an attempt to install a single national curriculum for high schools and another for colleges would surely fail. It tells you something when a principal piece of legislation meant to address this problem, the Civics Secures Democracy Act of 2021, explicitly states, "Nothing in this Act shall be construed to authorize the Secretary of Education to prescribe a civics and history curriculum." But the time is right to have a debate over making civics required and to determine what might constitute a curriculum that would be both useful and broadly acceptable. It is difficult to imagine a more urgent and critical need if American democracy is to survive.

OBLIGATION X

Put Country First

The Tenth Amendment to the Constitution, the final amendment of the Bill of Rights, is something of a catchall. "The powers not delegated to the United States by the Constitution, nor prohibited by it to the states, are reserved to the states respectively, or to the people." It follows on the nine previous amendments, which are for the most part specific in the rights they are protecting. The Tenth implies that there are additional rights the federal government cannot take away from the states and the people even though they may not be specified.

I say this because the nine previous obligations put forward in this book—Be Informed, Get Involved, Stay Open to Compromise, Remain Civil, Reject Violence, Value Norms, Promote the Common Good, Respect Government Service, and Support the Teaching of Civics—lead to a tenth that provides guidance for all other behaviors not already specified. I speak of the obligation to put the country and American democracy before party and person. This obligation is a thread that helps bind the fabric of this society and is an essential element of patriotism. Putting democracy and the country founded on it first is the only way to preserve and, better yet, improve a United States of America that for any and all of its shortcomings and flaws is still the most successful political experiment in human history and the one with the greatest potential. As he did so often, Abraham Lincoln said it best: "We shall nobly save, or meanly lose, the last best hope of earth."

What is required for this to happen more than anything else is an abundance of character, what in earlier times was known as virtue. James Madison, a founding father and the country's fourth president, was explicit on its centrality to the democratic project: "To suppose that any form of government will secure liberty or happiness without any virtue in the people, is a chimerical idea." Some two centuries later, the forty-third president of the United States, George W. Bush, made a similar point. "The public interest depends on private character, on integrity and tolerance toward others and the rule of conscience in our own lives. Self-government relies, in the end, on the governing of the self."

Virtue or character cannot be mandated or legislated. It can be encouraged on the basis that it is right and moral and ethical. But it can also be encouraged on practical cost-benefit, or instrumental, grounds, in that over time individuals and groups will be better off if they go about their lives keeping in mind broader and longer-term considerations.

The case of Merrick Garland is relevant here. Barack Obama nominated Garland, a respected and qualified court of appeals judge, to the Supreme Court in March 2016, two months into Obama's eighth and final year as president. The Republican-controlled Senate refused to take up, much less approve, the nomination even though several nominees to the court had been confirmed in the final year of presidential terms in the course of American history. Adding insult to injury was the Republican action four years later—when Republicans controlled both the White House and the Senate—in nominating and confirming Amy Coney Barrett to the Supreme Court just six weeks before the election that Donald Trump lost.

The danger is that these episodes will reinforce the already widely held view, which gained ground in 2000 as a result of the Supreme Court's ruling in the disputed Florida recount of the Bush-Gore vote, that the country's highest court is motivated more by political than legal considerations. The risk is that future Court opinions will not be respected or accepted by many Americans. It is advisable that Court decisions be guided by the principles of stare decisis—that things decided should stay decided unless there is a very good reason for change—and judicial restraint: if it is not necessary to decide more to dispose of a case, then it is necessary not to decide more. The Supreme Court violated both principles when it ruled in June 2022 to overturn *Roe v. Wade*, the 1973 decision that recognized a woman's right (derived from the Fourteenth Amendment) to have an abortion under defined circumstances. There was no valid reason justifying the opinion, while those bringing the case were not requesting that *Roe* be overturned but amended to narrow the period in which abortions could be legally carried out. What changed was that there was a new majority on the Court (brought about by the questionable political means just described) that sought to alter policy, in this instance by granting state governments vast power to regulate abortions. That this ruling came on the heels of another Supreme Court decision that limited the ability of states to regulate access to guns only added to the perception that politics more than the law was driving Court actions.

Already there are calls to increase the number of justices on the Supreme Court to create a new majority. The problem is that such "court-packing" by Democrats in retaliation for Republican hypocrisy in the Senate might provoke additional efforts to alter the Court's composition or independence that would further diminish faith in the Court and the legitimacy of its rulings. One could even imagine state legislatures mimicking what happened in the run-up to the Civil War and voting to nullify (or invalidate) the application of Supreme Court decisions in highly controversial areas such as gun control or abortion rights. A stable democracy requires institutions that enjoy widespread acceptance, and a stable American democracy requires a Supreme Court that enjoys sufficient standing so that its opinions even on the most controversial issues are broadly accepted as legitimate and final. Such standing has been seriously jeopardized.

When I was teaching in the 1980s at Harvard's John F. Kennedy School of Government, such calculations came under the heading of "thinking institutionally." The idea was to encourage students to think beyond the immediate issue at hand and short-term considerations and instead to think long-term, about how whatever institution was involved would benefit over time from certain behaviors, even if the individual did not support or benefit from the specific decision at hand.

Thinking institutionally has another dimension. Institutions are desirable because they encourage and lock in sought-after behaviors. Implicit in this notion is that doing the right thing, acting in a manner consistent with the obligations put forward in this book, will not just happen by itself. What gave rise to conservatism in the classic sense is that human nature required certain guardrails if our better angels were to prevail. Early on in the book the point was made that democracy does not inevitably materialize nor is it guaranteed to survive. A democratic society made up of individuals prepared to live by the obligations put forward here is far more likely to institutionalize democracy.

It is noteworthy that the concept of thinking institutionally was associated with a school named for John F. Kennedy, as the idea of doing the right thing even at personal cost formed the core of his book *Profiles in Courage*. First published in 1956, the book—attributed to then senator Kennedy but written in large part by his principal speechwriter Theodore Sorensen—tells the stories of eight U.S. senators who did the unpopular thing by standing up for compromise or principle when doing so put their careers at substantial risk. As Kennedy described it, "Some were courageous in their unyielding devotion to absolute principles; others were damned for advocating compromise." In many ways, he employs "courage" as a synonym for both virtue and character.

Particularly relevant for this book is what Kennedy goes on to say. "I am persuaded after long study of the record that the national interest, rather than private or political gain, furnished the basic motivation" for each of the eight senators he chose to write about. "His desire to win or maintain a reputation for integrity and courage was stronger than his desire to maintain his office." If there were to be a new edition of Kennedy's book, there would be a strong argument for a chapter on Representative Liz Cheney for risking her political future by what she said and did in the aftermath of January 6, 2021.

Sometimes it is easier to explain a point by highlighting its opposite. Here I would note the July 25, 2019, phone call between then president of the United States Donald Trump and Volodymyr Zelenskyy, the president of Ukraine. The latter asked for increased military aid, which Trump made conditional on Zelenskyy's launching an investigation of Joe Biden and his son that could prove politically useful for Trump. Trump later described the conversation as "perfect," but in reality, this placing of personal political interests before the country's national security was anything but.

Another way to think about what might be described as political character is suggested by the phrase "loyal opposition." Both words are essential. Let's begin with opposition. Democracy requires entities that are not members of the party controlling a branch of government (or, in the legislative branch, that are in the minority) that question it, hold it to account, and offer policy alternatives. This is what opposition is all about. It is unavoidable and necessary and constructive by keeping the majority honest and by creating the grounds for intelligent compromise.

But equally important is the other word in the phrase: loyal. The party in opposition has a higher loyalty to the law and to the success of the country. Opposition must be grounded in policy and principle, not politics, if the country is to succeed and democracy endure. To oppose, to block, when what is being put forward is preferable to any available alternative, is simply inconsistent with what is required of democracy. In return, the party in power is not meant to equate opposition with disloyalty. Members of the party in power, like those of the party out of power, must place the interests of the country before their own.

Politicians are unlikely to do so absent external pressure. It is far more likely that they will act appropriately if such behavior is rewarded and lesser behavior penalized. That is where the rest of us come in.

Conclusion

Speaking in 1932 at the Commonwealth Club in San Francisco, Democratic presidential nominee Franklin Delano Roosevelt put forward the proposition that "Government is a relation of give and take, a contract . . . rulers were accorded power, and the people consented to that power on consideration that they be accorded certain rights." Roosevelt was of course correct, but he did not go far enough.

The central argument of this book is that American democracy will endure only if obligations join rights at the core of a widely shared understanding of citizenship. By definition, obligations are behaviors that should happen but are not required as a matter of law. The motive for signing up to and practicing a set of obligations even when fulfilling them is not of direct or immediate benefit is because it will encourage behaviors, norms, relationships, and arrangements that over time will buttress our democracy and prove to be of benefit to ourselves, the society of which we are a member, and the country in which we are a citizen.

A report issued in 1945 meant to shape post–World War II education made much the same point: "Rugged individualism is not sufficient to constitute a democracy; democracy also is fraternity and cooperation for the common good. . . . When union is stressed to the exclusion of freedom we fall into totalitarianism; but when freedom is stressed exclusively we fall into chaos."

The call for a notion of citizenship that places obligations on an equal footing with rights is not intended to detract from the importance of respecting and protecting rights, which are central to a democracy. But rights viewed as absolutes and advanced in isolation from other considerations will risk the political system in which they are rooted. This is especially so as certain rights are in tension or even conflict, and if they are pursued without compromise, they will lead to political or physical conflict, an outcome that would leave the overall condition of rights far worse off.

Strengthening the collective acceptance of obligations will not happen on its own. I would like to think that the arguments informing this book are so compelling that elected and appointed officials would see the light and mend their ways. Alas, even I harbor no such illusions. Human nature, human foibles, are what they are.

But just as war is too important to be left to the generals, politics are too important to be left to the politicians. Citizens have to demand that those they vote for and support politically embrace the obligations put forward in these pages. To put it bluntly, political leaders disinclined to put country and American democracy before party or self will be persuaded to change their ways and do what is in the best interest of American democracy only if voters and funders reward those who act in a manner consistent with democracy and penalize those who do not. Politicians may not always be responsible, but they are almost always responsive.

Before going on, I want to address a path that might appeal to some readers: Why not make the Bill of Obligations amendments to the Constitution as was done with the Bill of Rights? The reality is that a majority of the obligations do not translate into legal requirements; obligations as defined and developed here are moral, not legal, undertakings. What is more, amending the Constitution is designed to be a difficult and slow-moving process. We do not have the luxury of time.

Some obligations, however, could potentially be translated into law. Legislation already introduced that sets parameters for—and dedicates resources to—national service and civics education could be passed and signed into law. Speaking of which, laws already exist prohibiting violence beyond self-defense. A legal system is in place to prosecute those accused of crimes, give them a fair trial, and fine or imprison them if they are found guilty. But most of the obligations set forth here seek to shape behavior, especially for how we deal with one another when inevitable differences arise, and cannot be required or mandated, only encouraged and rewarded.

This is not grounds for pessimism. In recent years we have seen voters hold politicians to account on single issues that matter most to them: gun control, abortion, taxes, education, and immigration to name a few. In 1994, Republicans advanced their "Contract with America" that expressed support for term limits and a balanced budget. It is arguably even more important to hold today's politicians to account on their commitment to democracy and the obligations so central to it. I tend to oppose single-issue litmus tests for determining political activity, but if there is to be one, let it be a candidate's or party's willingness to commit to acting in a democratic manner. Our support should go only to candidates who have clearly committed to their democratic obligations, namely rejecting violence, proposing policies grounded in facts, and accepting election results shown to be accurate.

Implicit in the above is that a commitment to the obligations on which democracy rests must, in times of division, take priority over other immediate policy concerns, whether it's lower taxes, an expanded safety net, abortion, guns, support for Israel, or just about anything else. These issues are critical, but we will cease to have meaningful debates or effective policies vis-à-vis any of them if we do not have a vibrant democracy. For this reason, the decision of several Democratic political groups to fund extremist Republican candidates who among other things had adopted positions inconsistent with upholding democracy was as short-sighted as it was cynical. We either place democracy first or it will not last.

But what will also be required is that those with significant influence in our society say and do more about the need for those they reach to embrace obligations. Employees, investors, and consumers are pressuring corporate leaders to adopt policies meant to slow climate change or promote diversity. Many of these same leaders sacrificed significant resources and revenues when they backed away from investments and operations in Russia following its February 2022 invasion of Ukraine. Ideally, these constituencies would pressure these same corporate leaders to adopt policies that promote democracy. This could include not advertising on networks or in publications that consistently peddle falsehoods or encourage violence.

Congregational and religious leaders have regular opportunities to preach what ought to be practiced. Doing so does not require taking stands on issues but a stand on behavior. The sacred texts central to religions contain a good deal of guidance here.

What took place with Spotify in early 2022 is a textbook case of democratic obligations ignored by some and embraced by others. The former applies to the company, which would not set meaningful standards of accuracy for its popular and lucrative podcast hosted by Joe Rogan. The musician Neil Young then demanded that Spotify either take down the podcast or he would no longer allow Spotify to carry his music. The company refused, and Young walked. Joni Mitchell; Crosby, Stills & Nash; and Brené Brown, among others, followed him out the door. The company, unlike these artists, would not put principle before profit. What will matter is how many more artists follow suit and how many listeners refuse to patronize Spotify, or other social media and cable networks that refuse to take responsibility for what they broadcast even when it weakens democracy.

Those who have formal powers, such as those in law enforcement and the military, likewise have a special responsibility to exercise those powers within the law and fairly. The population's willingness to live under and up to the rule of law depends on the maintenance of social order and the implementation of the law in a manner consistent with its letter and spirit.

Some final points. I mentioned in the discussion of the final obligation the notion of thinking institutionally. One objective for anyone working in an organization and, in particular, for those leading one is to leave it in better shape than you found it. "Better" can be measured by profit or impact or effectiveness or whatever is relevant. Much the same should hold for American democracy and for the United States. The goal, the commitment for us all, ought to be to hand off a country to our children and grandchildren that is in better shape than what we received from our parents and grandparents.

Some readers will no doubt take issue with one or more of the obligations put forward here; others will be disappointed that a particular obligation did not make the cut. That too can be a fruitful topic for discussion. What I hope is that this book stimulates conversations about citizenship and as a result alters the context in which American politics are conducted. It is no exaggeration to point out that the future of the country and indeed the world depend on it.

James Madison once said that "a bad cause seldom fails to betray itself." He may prove right, but those who cherish American democracy cannot count on it. The reality that January 6, and the subsequent revelations about efforts to impound voting machines and discount legally cast ballots, has failed to shock the body politic into its senses, has failed to stir us into action to protect and preserve this democracy, challenges the conventional wisdom that crises are automatic precursors of change. We get the government and the country we deserve. Getting the one we need, however, is up to us.

ACKNOWLEDGMENTS

Writing a book is a mostly solitary undertaking, although it is punctuated at important intervals with the involvement of others. And if you are as fortunate as I have been in the course of writing this book, these contributions are invaluable.

I will begin with those friends who read and commented on one or more drafts of this book. To Michael Beschloss, Eddie Glaude, Jon Meacham, and Jim Zirin, I offer my deep thanks and appreciation. It is an act of generosity and commitment to find and take the time to read and comment on a manuscript (in Jim's case more than once) and to critique both what is there and what is not but ought to be. We can debate whether the result is good, but what cannot be debated is that it is much better than it would have been without the input from these individuals.

I also want to thank three members of my immediate family

who read the manuscript, challenged me in conversation, or both. Here I include my wife, Susan Mercandetti, who brings to the enterprise insights gleaned from decades of experience as a world-class book and magazine editor, and our two children, Sam and Francesca Haass, who in addition to their keen intellects possess considerable political experience for their age. I owe them more than I can express for their love, support, and, not least, for putting up with me throughout the writing process. Kennan, who joined the family some two years ago, also merits a mention, as he was good enough not to eat any of my notes or manuscript pages but instead accompanied me on long walks that helped me work through the issues any writer faces.

A loud shout-out goes to my publishing team. This is the third book I have done with them, the "them" being my agent, Andrew Wylie, and my editors, Scott Moyers and Christopher Richards at Penguin Press. Scott has been and is a real intellectual partner. Along the way, Christopher decamped to Scribner, but the good news is that Natalie Coleman came on board. They all managed to challenge and support me at one and the same time. They also made a good many specific suggestions for which the manuscript is incomparably better.

Speaking of the team at Penguin Press, I want to thank Ryan Benitez, Elisabeth Calamari, Chelsea Cohen, Tyler Comrie, Alyson D'Amato, Tess Espinoza, Daniel Lagin, and Danielle Plafsky.

I want to express my deep appreciation as well to my colleagues here at the Council on Foreign Relations, to Team CFR. For a host of reasons I will begin with David Sacks. David, in addition to his own writing and research on matters ranging from Hans Morgenthau to Taiwan, found the time to provide detailed comments on multiple drafts of the manuscript. He served as an invaluable sounding board throughout. Jennifer Williams took the lead on research and providing me with the background material that informs much of the text and fills many of the notes. She too provided helpful feedback along the way to what I had written. Jim Lindsay (who heads our in-house think tank) and Yascha Mounk (who recently produced an important book of his own on democracy) read and provided thoughtful reactions to the draft. Doreen Bonnami read and commented on the book when she was not busy making sure my overfilled schedule somehow preserved time for writing. The same holds for my chief of staff, Jeff Reinke. And Iva Zoric, in addition to commenting on the manuscript, worked hard to make sure this book was not the proverbial tree falling in the forest that nobody noticed but rather garnered the attention the subject deserves.

I want and need to say something else about the Council on Foreign Relations. I would be remiss if I did not point out it is an independent, nonpartisan membership organization, think tank, publisher, and educator. Just over one hundred years old, the CFR endeavors to be a resource that adds to the quality of the debate in this country and around the world about the foreign policy choices facing governments and citizens. I will forever be grateful for the opportunity to serve for two decades as its president and work with such an extraordinary staff, board, and membership. The Council does not, however, take positions of its own on matters of policy, and what is contained in these pages represents my thinking, not the institution's.

WHERE TO GO FOR MORE

As you can readily see, this section is titled "Where to Go for More," but it just as easily could be called "How to Become and Remain an Informed Citizen." The place to start is with the essential documents: the Declaration of Independence, the Articles of Confederation, and the Constitution, all of which are available at www.archives.gov. Next, I would suggest *The Federalist Papers*, the eighty-five essays authored individually by James Madison, Alexander Hamilton, and John Jay and published in 1787 and 1788 under the collective pseudonym of Publius. Blending analysis and advocacy, the essays succeeded in their original aim of garnering public support for the proposed Constitution—and over the more than two centuries since have become an enduring classic of political philosophy.

Staying with writings that have stood the test of time, I would also recommend that everyone read Alexis de Tocqueville's *Democracy in America*. Published in 1835, it is filled with timeless insights into what might be described as the American political character and retains great influence in part because it is so widely read. Less well known but also valuable is *The American Commonwealth*, written half a century later by James Bryce. It is revealing but perhaps not surprising that both these books were written by outsiders, by a Frenchman and a Scot, respectively. They make for a good reminder that others see us differently but often more clearly than we see ourselves.

I would then suggest delving into history. There are far too many excellent books on the various phases of American history to mention, but some that I have found most memorable over the years include James McPherson on the Civil War (*Battle Cry of Freedom: The Civil War Era*), Richard Hofstadter's *The Age of Reform* as well as his *The American Political Tradition: And the Men Who Made It*, and Barbara Tuchman's *The Proud Tower*. Books that take a larger sweep of this country's past include Howard Zinn's *A People's History of the United States*, Paul Johnson's *A History of the American People*, and, most recently, the volume by Jill Lepore, *These Truths: A History of the United States*.

One can and should take a deeper dive into specific critical parts of this country's past. I am not an expert on these subjects, but based on my own reading experience and after talking with others, I have assembled a partial list: Dee Brown, *Bury My Heart at Wounded Knee: An Indian History of the American West*; Peter

Kolchin, *American Slavery: 1619–1877*; Henry Louis Gates Jr., *Stony the Road: Reconstruction, White Supremacy, and the Rise of Jim Crow*; Tina Cassidy, *Mr. President, How Long Must We Wait?: Alice Paul, Woodrow Wilson, and the Fight for the Right to Vote*; Taylor Branch, *Parting the Waters: America in the King Years, 1954–63*; and Annette Gordon-Reed, *On Juneteenth*. I would also recommend reading writings by or about some of the pivotal figures in the fight for political equality, such as Frederick Douglass, W.E.B. Du Bois, Susan B. Anthony, and Martin Luther King Jr.

A separate category of books focuses less on a particular period than on what might be described as enduring political features of this country. Here I would mention Samuel P. Huntington's *American Politics: The Promise of Disharmony*, Richard Neustadt's *Presidential Power and the Modern Presidents: The Politics of Leadership from Roosevelt to Reagan*, and almost any book by Arthur M. Schlesinger Jr. (in particular his *The Cycles of American History*). I would also recommend Gordon Wood, *Power and Liberty: Constitutionalism in the American Revolution*; Robert A. Dahl, *Democracy and Its Critics*; Akhil Reed Amar, *The Words That Made Us: America's Constitutional Conversation, 1760–1840*; Gabriel A. Almond and Sidney Verba, *The Civic Culture*; and the personal book by Danielle Allen, *Talking to Strangers: Anxieties of Citizenship Since Brown v. Board of Education*.

In the course of writing this book, I did something I had never done before that I now recommend to you: go back and read speeches by the presidents, above all their inaugural and farewell addresses. They are readily available on the Internet. Not all are memorable, much less poetic, but a few are one or the other or both, and every one is valuable as a window on the moment it was delivered. And since Lincoln was robbed by an assassin of the chance to give a farewell address, I would suggest you read and reread his Gettysburg Address. It is the best example I know of that less is often more.

Speaking of presidents, their memoirs can make for rich reading, as can many biographies, some of which are not just good but great. When it comes to the latter, you would be hard-pressed to go wrong if the author's name happens to be Beschloss, Caro, Kearns Goodwin, McCullough, Meacham, Logevall, Reeves, or Schlesinger. There is as well the series of consistently good volumes (some forty-two at last count) on the American presidents published by Times Books.

I also read quite a few Supreme Court decisions in the course of writing this book. I am not trained as a lawyer, but they often make for compelling reading. Dissents can be as or even more illuminating than the majority opinion. You can find the texts of Court opinions at www.supremecourt.gov.

Recent developments affecting this country and its democracy have stimulated a host of thoughtful volumes. Some of those I found to be most insightful were Ezra Klein's *Why We're Polarized*; George Packer's *Last Best Hope: America in Crisis and Renewal*; Evan Osnos's *Wildland: The Making of America's Fury*;

Yascha Mounk's *The Great Experiment: Why Diverse Democracies Fall Apart and How They Can Endure*; Suzanne Mettler and Robert Lieberman's *Four Threats: The Recurring Crises of American Democracy*; Steven Levitsky and Daniel Ziblatt's *How Democracies Die*; Bill Bishop and Robert Cushing's *The Big Sort: Why the Clustering of Like-Minded America Is Tearing Us Apart*; and Michael Sandel's *Democracy's Discontent: America in Search of a Public Philosophy*. I also suggest you read the January/February 2022 issue of the *Atlantic*. For contrast, and decidedly more upbeat, is Robert Putnam's *The Upswing: How America Came Together a Century Ago and How We Can Do It Again*. The public hearings held by the Select Committee to Investigate the January 6th Attack on the United States Capitol should be required viewing and are readily available online.

There is considerable material dealing with the basics of civics online, beginning with iCivics (www.icivics.org) and the National Constitution Center, which offer free classes on civics (www.constitutioncenter.org/interactive-constitution/online -civic-learning-opportunities). Common Sense Education has a list of tools and websites that help supplement teaching civics (www .commonsense.org/education/top-picks/best-government-and -civics-websites-and-games). And Khan Academy offers a free American civics course (www.khanacademy.org/humanities /us-government-and-civics/american-civics-parent). I would also recommend the Leonore Annenberg Institute for Civics (www

.annenbergpublicpolicycenter.org/political-communication
/leonore-annenberg-institute-for-civics). You can also try your
hand at the test questions given to those who want to become
American citizens, which can be found at www.uscis.gov/sites
/default/files/document/flash-cards/M-638_red.pdf.

Staying up to date requires time and effort of a different sort.
There is no substitute for regular (daily) reading of a good newspaper such as the *New York Times*, the *Washington Post*, or the
Wall Street Journal. All are home to several quality columnists
who write editorials that are worth reading; just be sure you distinguish between all of these and what runs on the news pages.
Some of the regional papers I would also recommend include (but
are in no way limited to) the *Los Angeles Times*, the *Boston Globe*,
the *Philadelphia Inquirer*, the *Chicago Tribune*, and the *Miami Her-
ald*. More generally, local newspapers can also be valuable when
it comes to state and local politics. Ideally your local paper makes
use of reputable news services such as the Associated Press or
Reuters to supplement what they themselves can do. There are as
well *The Hill* and *USA Today*, both of which cover politics.

The daily curation of articles from far and wide by my friend
John Ellis (News Items) that is available on Substack is well worth
subscribing to. And speaking of Substack, I also invariably learn
when I read Heather Cox Richardson's daily reflections on politics
and history. *Politico* and *Axios* put out valuable daily newsletters.
It is always dangerous to single out one person, but I will ignore

my own caution and say that for several years now I have found the most insightful writings about many of the issues covered in this book are by Thomas Edsall in the *New York Times*. Certain magazines are also excellent. *The Economist* provides the best one-stop shopping each week. *The New Yorker* and the *Atlantic* frequently publish important pieces.

As for television and radio, the most substantive and balanced coverage of politics can usually be found on PBS (*NewsHour*) and NPR (*Morning Edition*, *All Things Considered*, *Weekend Edition*). I am biased, as I appear on it with some frequency, but I would argue *Morning Joe* on MSNBC often provides the best conversation weekday mornings about things political. The Sunday shows on the networks and cable also can be important to catch. C-SPAN offers invaluable coverage of congressional hearings, political events, and speeches. Last but not least are podcasts. The three I would highlight are *The Daily* produced by the *New York Times*, *Up First* by NPR, and the daily podcast from the *Economist*. What also matters on all of the above is that you go to multiple sources that ideally reflect various perspectives. Back in the day when I frequented a gym I used to divide the time on the elliptical machine among CNN, Fox, and MSNBC—at least the time I wasn't devoting to ESPN.

I can't resist the temptation to add a brief section on political fiction. Truth may be stranger than fiction, but fiction can still be illuminating, not to mention enjoyable. My own list includes Allen

Drury, *Advise and Consent*; Robert Penn Warren, *All the King's Men*; Harper Lee, *To Kill a Mockingbird*; George Orwell, *1984*; Gore Vidal, *Washington, D.C.*; Sinclair Lewis, *It Can't Happen Here*. I am also a big fan of the books and short stories of Ward Just. My son came of age watching *The West Wing*, and I loved both the riotously funny if cynical book and British TV series *Yes, Minister*. And, even if it is not a substitute for reading *The Federalist Papers*, you would be hard pressed to spend a more enjoyable evening than watching the musical *Hamilton*.

International perspectives (and perspectives on international developments) are likewise essential for the informed citizen. The website of Project Syndicate (project-syndicate.org, for whom I write a monthly column) offers a valuable collection of opinion pieces by writers from all over the world. The BBC website (bbc.com) is a wonderful news resource, as is that of the *Financial Times* (ft.com). I would also recommend the website of the Council on Foreign Relations (cfr.org) and that of *Foreign Affairs* magazine (foreignaffairs.com) for analysis of U.S. foreign policy and global issues. Please do not dismiss this advice even if the fact that I work where I work makes what I say suspect here.

One last thing. This entire section has been devoted to things you can and should read and hear. Let me also suggest what you can experience. Go visit any of the presidential libraries or the National Archives. Watch or better yet sit in on a committee hearing of Congress or your state legislature. Go to the local school board meeting. Attend oral arguments at the Supreme Court. Walk a Civil War battlefield. Do not skip out on serving on a jury. You will come away with a new appreciation of how we got to where we are and why what is best about this country is worth preserving.

NOTES

Preface

xii **a plurality (21 percent) believe:** Mark Murray, "NBC News Poll: 57% of Voters Say Investigations into Trump Should Continue," NBC News, August 21, 2022, https://www.nbcnews.com/meet-the-press/first-read /nbc-news-poll-57-voters-say-investigations-trump-continue-rcna 43989.

xii **There is overwhelming evidence:** We continue to learn more about January 6 and President Trump's involvement in the insurrection. For reporting on the administration's involvement in events and the assistance certain congressmen provided, see Jonathan Martin and Alexander Burns, *This Will Not Pass: Trump, Biden, and the Battle for America's Future* (New York: Simon & Schuster, 2022); Luke Broadwater and Alan Feuer, "New Details Underscore House G.O.P. Role in Jan. 6 Planning," *New York Times*, April 26, 2022, https://www.nytimes.com/2022/04/26 /us/politics/jan-6-texts-mark-meadows.html; Kyle Cheney and Nicholas Wu, "GOP Lawmakers Were Deeply Involved in Trump Plans to Overturn Election, New Evidence Suggests," *Politico*, April 23, 2022, https://

www.politico.com/news/2022/04/22/gop-lawmakers-deeply-involved
-in-trump-plans-to-overturn-election-new-evidence-suggests
-00027340. On President Trump's involvement, see Luke Broadwater
and Alan Feuer, "Filing Provides New Details on Trump White House
Planning for Jan. 6," *New York Times*, April 23, 2022, https://www
.nytimes.com/2022/04/23/us/politics/trump-meadows-freedom
-caucus-jan-6.html.

xiii **erosion of popular support:** Michael Albertus and Guy Grossman,
"Americans Are Officially Giving Up on Democracy," *Foreign Policy*,
October 16, 2020, https://foreignpolicy.com/2020/10/16/americans
-are-officially-giving-up-on-democracy; Matthew S. Schwartz, "1 in 4
Americans Say Violence Against the Government Is Sometimes OK,"
NPR, January 31, 2022, https://www.npr.org/2022/01/31/1076873172
/one-in-four-americans-say-violence-against-the-government-is
-sometimes-okay.

xiv **"The development of a stable":** Gabriel A. Almond and Sidney Verba,
The Civic Culture: Political Attitudes and Democracy in Five Nations
(Newbury Park, CA: SAGE Publications, 1989), 366.

xv **"habits of citizenship":** Danielle S. Allen, *Talking to Strangers: Anxieties
of Citizenship Since Brown v. Board of Education* (Chicago: University of
Chicago Press, 2004).

xvi **"that all men are created equal":** The full text of the Declaration of
Independence can be found at https://www.archives.gov/founding-docs
/declaration-transcript.

xvii **"democracy is the worst form":** Winston Churchill, speech before the
House of Commons, November 11, 1947, as quoted in Richard Lang-
worth (ed.), *Churchill by Himself: The Definitive Collection of Quotations*
(New York: PublicAffairs, 2008), 574.

xvii **overwhelming majority of Americans:** For instance, a recent poll found
that only 7 percent of Republicans and 6 percent of Democrats "strongly
favor" dividing the United States into two countries, while 68 percent of
Democrats and 65 percent of Republicans "strongly oppose" this idea.
"Exclusive: TNR's Democracy Poll," *The New Republic*, May 2022. Yet in
June 2022, following the Texas Republican convention, the Report of the

Permanent 2022 Platform & Resolutions Committee included the following language regarding Texas independence: "We urge the Texas Legislature to pass bill [*sic*] in its next session requiring a referendum in the 2023 general election for the people of Texas to determine whether or not the State of Texas should reassert its status as an independent nation." https://texasgop.org/wp-content/uploads/2022/06/6-Permanent -Platform-Committee-FINAL-REPORT-6-16-2022.pdf.

xvii **"Our nation can be strong abroad":** Jimmy Carter, "Inaugural Address" (speech, Washington, D.C., January 20, 1977), The Jimmy Carter Presidential Library, https://www.jimmycarterlibrary.gov/assets/docu ments/speeches/inaugadd.phtml.

xviii **As I argued in a book:** Richard N. Haass, *Foreign Policy Begins at Home: The Case for Putting America's House in Order* (New York: Basic Books, 2013).

xviii **Chinese television was filled with images:** Tracy Wen Liu, "Chinese Media Calls Capitol Riot 'World Masterpiece,'" *Foreign Policy*, January 8, 2021, https://foreignpolicy.com/2021/01/08/chinese-media-calls-capitol -riot-world-masterpiece.

xviii **likely be the principal beneficiaries:** Larry Diamond, "A World Without American Democracy?," *Foreign Affairs*, July 2, 2021, https://www .foreignaffairs.com/articles/americas/2021-07-02/world-without -american-democracy.

PART ONE: THE CRISIS OF OUR RIGHTS-BASED DEMOCRACY

Rights and Their Limits

3 **There is also the danger:** James Madison, *Federalist*, No. 51, February 6, 1788, Founders Online, National Archives, https://founders.archives.gov /documents/Hamilton/01-04-02-0199.

4 **"in order to form":** The full text of the U.S. Constitution can be found at https://www.archives.gov/founding-docs/constitution-transcript.

4 **"Each state retains":** The full text of the Articles of Confederation can

be found at https://www.archives.gov/milestone-documents/articles
-of-confederation.

5 **"firm league of friendship":** *Articles of Confederation*, Article III.

5 **There were splits:** Gordon S. Wood, *Power and Liberty: Constitutionalism in the American Revolution* (Oxford: Oxford University Press, 2021).

6 **James Madison concluded:** James Madison, "Notes of Debates in the Federal Convention of 1787," *Legislative Records*, June 30, 1787.

6 **In Madison's view:** *Federalist*, No. 51, February 6, 1788.

7 **moved to the executive branch:** Arthur M. Schlesinger Jr., *The Imperial Presidency* (New York: Houghton Mifflin, 1973); Michael Beschloss, *Presidents of War: The Epic Story, from 1807 to Modern Times* (New York: Crown, 2018).

8 **incontestably the weakest:** *Federalist*, No. 78, May 28, 1788, Founders Online, National Archives, https://founders.archives.gov/documents /Hamilton/01-04-02-0241.

8 **established the ability of the courts:** *Marbury v. Madison*, 5 U.S. 137 (1805).

8 **"Give me liberty":** Patrick Henry, "Give Me Liberty or Give Me Death" (speech, Richmond, Virginia, March 23, 1775), The Avalon Project, Yale Law School, https://avalon.law.yale.edu/18th_century/patrick.asp.

8 **"This Constitution is said to have":** Patrick Henry, "Speech Before Virginia Ratifying Convention" (speech, Richmond, Virginia, June 5, 1788), Teaching American History, https://teachingamericanhistory.org /document/patrick-henry-virginia-ratifying-convention-va.

9 **Bill of Rights became:** The full text of the Bill of Rights can be found at https://www.archives.gov/founding-docs/bill-of-rights-transcript; it is worth noting, however, that a Bill of Rights was itself controversial. Alexander Hamilton, for one, argued that it was "unnecessary" and "even dangerous." *Federalist*, No. 84, May 28, 1788, Founders Online, National Archives, https://founders.archives.gov/documents/Hamilton /01-04-02-0247.

10 **so-called three-fifths compromise:** U.S. Const., art. I, § 2.

11 **enslaved persons could be brought:** U.S. Const., art. I, § 9.

11 **fugitive slaves be returned:** U.S. Const., art. IV, § 2.

11 **"The Civil War resolved":** Michael J. Sandel, *Democracy's Discontent* (Cambridge: The Belknap Press of Harvard University Press, 1998), 39.

11 **"no State shall make":** U.S. Const., amend. XIV.

12 **the nation's "unfinished work":** Abraham Lincoln, "Gettysburg Address" (speech, Gettysburg, Pennsylvania, November 19, 1863), available at Cornell University, https://rmc.library.cornell.edu/gettysburg/good _cause/transcript.htm.

13 **Roosevelt called "freedom from want":** Franklin Delano Roosevelt, "Annual Message (Four Freedoms) to Congress" (speech, Washington, D.C., January 6, 1941), National Archives, https://www.archives.gov /milestone-documents/president-franklin-roosevelts-annual-message -to-congress.

15 **"Many of our cases":** Stephen Breyer, "Making Our Democracy Work: A Judge's View" (speech, Kansas City, Missouri, December 8, 2011), The Kansas City Public Library, https://www.youtube.com/watch?v=EME 0fQDpWgw.

15 **Brandeis once described "sunlight":** Louis Brandeis "What Publicity Can Do," *Harpers Weekly*, December 20, 1913, https://www.sechistorical .org/collection/papers/1910/1913_12_20_What_Publicity_Ca.pdf.

16 **debate over the "social contract":** The term was initially articulated and developed by the Enlightenment philosopher Jean-Jacques Rousseau in his 1762 book *The Social Contract*.

16 **"It is not enough to talk":** Max Arzt, *Justice and Mercy: Commentary on the Liturgy of the New Year and The Day of Atonement* (New York: Holt Rinehart Winston, 1963), 183.

Democratic Deterioration

17 **But is that true?:** Robert Kagan, "Our Constitutional Crisis Is Already Here," *Washington Post*, September 23, 2021, https://www.washington post.com/opinions/2021/09/23/robert-kagan-constitutional-crisis; Martin Wolf, "The Strange Death of American Democracy," *Financial Times*, September 28, 2021, https://www.ft.com/content/a2e499d0-10f0 -4fa2-8243-e23eedc4f9f4; Barton Gellman, "Trump's Next Coup Has Al-

ready Begun," *Atlantic*, January/February 2022, https://www.theatlantic
.com/magazine/archive/2022/01/january-6-insurrection-trump-coup
-2024-election/620843.

19 **insisted despite an absence:** As of mid-2022, President Trump and
many Republican leaders continue to claim the election was fraudulent: Olivia Beavers and Nicholas Wu, "1 Year Later, GOP Still Chained to
Trump's Baseless Election Fraud Claims," *Politico*, November 3, 2021,
https://www.politico.com/news/2021/11/03/gop-trump-baseless
-election-fraud-claims-518603. The courts have ruled on numerous
occasions that there was no fraud: Jan Wolfe, "Factbox: Trump's False
Claims Debunked: The 2020 Election and Jan. 6 Riot," Reuters, January 6,
2022, https://www.reuters.com/world/us/trumps-false-claims-debunked
-2020-election-jan-6-riot-2022-01-06. In addition, the Associated Press
found no statistically significant election fraud: Christina A. Cassidy,
"Far Too Little Vote Fraud to Tip Election to Trump, AP Finds," AP News,
December 14, 2021, https://apnews.com/article/voter-fraud-election
-2020-joe-biden-donald-trump-7fcb6f134e528fee8237c7601db3328f.

19 **democratic backsliding, a trend worldwide:** Freedom House, "Freedom
in the World 2022," February 2022, https://freedomhouse.org/sites
/default/files/2022-02/FIW_2022_PDF_Booklet_Digital_Final_Web
.pdf; Larry Diamond, *Ill Winds: Saving Democracy from Russian Rage,
Chinese Ambition, and American Complacency* (New York: Penguin
Press, 2019).

19 **significant percentage of the population:** For instance, a December
2021 poll found that of 1,000 respondents, only 58 percent believed that
Joe Biden's electoral victory was legitimate, with more than a fifth saying that it was "definitely not legitimate." Tatishe Nteta, "One Year
Later, New UMass Amherst Poll Finds Continued National Political Division over the Jan. 6 Attack on the U.S. Capitol," University of Massachusetts Amherst, December 28, 2021, https://www.umass.edu/news/article
/one-year-later-new-umass-amherst-poll-finds-continued-national
-political-division-over; Joel Rose and Liz Baker, "6 in 10 Americans
Say U.S. Democracy Is in Crisis as the 'Big Lie' Takes Root," NPR, January 3, 2022, https://www.npr.org/2022/01/03/1069764164/american

-democracy-poll-jan-6; Beavers and Wu, "1 Year Later, GOP Still Chained to Trump's Baseless Election Fraud Claims."

20 **George Washington warned:** In his farewell address, President Washington warned, "The alternate domination of one faction over another, sharpened by the spirit of revenge natural to party dissension, which in different ages and countries has perpetrated the most horrid enormities, is itself a frightful despotism. But this leads at length to a more formal and permanent despotism . . . and sooner or later the chief of some prevailing faction, more able or more fortunate than his competitors, turns this disposition to the purposes of his own elevation on the ruins of public liberty." George Washington, *Copy of Washington's Farewell Address*, U.S. Senate, https://www.senate.gov/artandhistory /history/resources/pdf/Washingtons_Farewell_Address.pdf.

20 **"a number of citizens":** James Madison, *Federalist*, No. 10, Founders Online, National Archives, https://founders.archives.gov/documents /Madison/01-10-02-0178.

20 **increasingly partisan, dysfunctional politics:** Jennifer McCoy and Benjamin Press, "What Happens When Democracies Become Perniciously Polarized?," Carnegie Endowment for International Peace, January 18, 2022, https://carnegieendowment.org/2022/01/18/what-happens -when-democracies-become-perniciously-polarized-pub-86190. Voting patterns for Supreme Court nominees offer an interesting case study regarding the increasing partisanship in the United States. Chief Justice John Roberts, who was nominated by a Republican president, received twenty-two Democratic votes, but the seven justices nominated since then have each received fewer than ten votes from the opposing party (not a single Democrat supported Amy Coney Barrett's nomination). Peter Baker, "Battle Over Abortion Threatens to Deepen America's Divide," *New York Times*, May 6, 2022, https://www.nytimes.com/2022 /05/06/us/politics/abortion-rights-supreme-court-roe-v-wade.html.

21 **could not even agree:** House Republican leadership rejected the idea of establishing a bipartisan commission modeled on the 9/11 Commission, which Senate Republicans subsequently blocked. As a result, House Democrats passed a resolution to create a special investigative

committee, which required only a simple majority vote. Only two House Republicans voted in favor of the resolution. Jacqueline Alemany and Tom Hamburger, "The Jan. 6 Committee: What It Has Done and Where It Is Headed," *Washington Post*, January 4, 2022, https://www.washington post.com/politics/2022/01/04/january-6-committee-explainer.

21 **Fewer bills become law:** For instance, according to one report, 233 substantive bills were enacted in 2019–2020, compared with 408 in 1989–1990 and 463 in 1999–2000. Drew DeSilver, "Nothing Lame about This Lame Duck: 116th Congress Had Busiest Post-Election Session in Recent History," Pew Research Center, January 21, 2021, https://www.pewresearch .org/fact-tank/2021/01/21/nothing-lame-about-this-lame-duck-116th -congress-had-busiest-post-election-session-in-recent-history.

21 **violence supported or at least tolerated:** Jonathan Martin and Alexander Burns, *This Will Not Pass: Trump, Biden, and the Battle for America's Future* (New York: Simon & Schuster, 2022); Jonathan Weisman and Reid J. Epstein, "G.O.P. Declares Jan. 6 Attack 'Legitimate Political Discourse,'" *New York Times*, February 4, 2022, https://www.nytimes.com /2022/02/04/us/politics/republicans-jan-6-cheney-censure.html.

21 **call on the military to impound:** Matthew S. Schwartz, "Jan. 6 Panel Is Investigating a Trump Administration Plan to Seize Voting Machines," NPR, January 23, 2022, https://www.npr.org/2022/01/23/1075219215 /jan-6-panel-is-investigating-a-trump-administration-plan-to-seize -voting-machine.

21 **rejected by tens of millions of Americans:** PRRI Staff, "Competing Visions of America: An Evolving Identity or a Culture Under Attack? Findings from the 2021 American Values Survey," Public Religion Research Institute, November 1, 2021, https://www.prri.org/research/competing-visions-of-america-an-evolving-identity-or-a-culture-under-attack.

21 **In Georgia, a law:** Nick Corasaniti and Reid J. Epstein, "What Georgia's Voting Law Really Does," *New York Times*, last updated August 18, 2021, https://www.nytimes.com/2021/04/02/us/politics/georgia-voting-law -annotated.html.

22 **form of a second civil war:** David Remnick, "Is a Civil War Ahead?," *New Yorker*, January 5, 2022, https://www.newyorker.com/news/daily

-comment/is-a-civil-war-ahead; Michelle Goldberg, "Are We Really Facing a Second Civil War?," *New York Times*, January 6, 2022, https://www.nytimes.com/2022/01/06/opinion/america-civil-war.html; Paul D. Eaton, Antonio M. Taguba, and Steven M. Anderson, "3 Retired Generals: The Military Must Prepare Now for a 2024 Insurrection," *Washington Post*, December 17, 2021, https://www.washingtonpost.com/opinions/2021/12/17/eaton-taguba-anderson-generals-military.

22 **acts of violence by and among:** For instance, the leaders of the January 6 insurrection harnessed social media to organize. Craig Timberg, Elizabeth Dwoskin, and Reed Albergotti, "Inside Facebook, Jan. 6 Violence Fueled Anger, Regret over Missed Warning Signs," *Washington Post*, October 22, 2021, https://www.washingtonpost.com/technology/2021/10/22/jan-6-capitol-riot-facebook; Barbara F. Walter, *How Civil Wars Start: And How to Stop them* (New York: Crown, 2022).

22 **Northern Ireland and the Troubles:** I say this in part because of my own involvement with Northern Ireland, first as U.S. envoy to the Northern Ireland peace process from 2001 to 2003 and then as chair of the multiparty negotiations in Northern Ireland in 2013. For more on this period, see Richard English, *Armed Struggle: The History of the IRA* (Oxford: Oxford University Press, 2003), and Patrick Radden Keefe, *Say Nothing: A True Story of Murder and Memory in Northern Ireland* (New York: Doubleday, 2019).

23 **a woman reportedly asked Benjamin Franklin:** Josh Levy, "'A Republic If You Can Keep It': Elizabeth Willing Powel, Benjamin Franklin, and the James McHenry Journal," Library of Congress, January 6, 2022, https://blogs.loc.gov/manuscripts/2022/01/a-republic-if-you-can-keep-it-elizabeth-willing-powel-benjamin-franklin-and-the-james-mchenry-journal.

23 **"Democracy never lasts long":** John Adams, "From John Adams to John Taylor, 17 December 1814," Founders Online, National Archives, https://founders.archives.gov/documents/Adams/99-02-02-6371.

23 **"If destruction be our lot":** Abraham Lincoln, "The Perpetuation of Our Political Institutions: Address Before the Young Men's Lyceum of Springfield, Illinois," January 27, 1838, https://www.abrahamlincolnonline.org/lincoln/speeches/lyceum.htm.

24 **"Since the end of the Cold War":** Steven Levitsky and Daniel Ziblatt, *How Democracies Die* (New York: Crown, 2018), 4.

24 **what seems to matter most:** Juan J. Linz, *The Breakdown of Democratic Regimes* (Baltimore: Johns Hopkins University Press, 1978).

25 **"Things fall apart":** William Butler Yeats, "The Second Coming," 1920, available at https://www.poetryfoundation.org/poems/43290/the-second -coming.

25 **"Freedom and democracy and the rule of law":** Amy B. Wang, "'A Force for Good': Biden and Other Political Stars Eulogize Albright," *Washington Post*, April 27, 2022, https://www.washingtonpost.com/politics/2022 /04/27/madeleine-albright-funeral.

26 **democratic reforms are in peril:** Ryan C. Berg and Lauri Tähtinen, "Latin America's Democratic Recession," *Foreign Affairs*, October 6, 2021, https://www.foreignaffairs.com/articles/central-america-caribbean /2021-10-06/latin-americas-democratic-recession; Daniel Zovatto, "The Rapidly Deteriorating Quality of Democracy in Latin America," Brookings Institution, February 28, 2020, https://www.brookings.edu/blog/order -from-chaos/2020/02/28/the-rapidly-deteriorating-quality-of-democracy -in-latin-america.

26 **losing ground to parties:** Gideon Rachman, "Democracy in Europe Adjusts to the Far Right," *Financial Times*, June 28, 2021, https://www.ft .com/content/8dded432-2d6d-4ee7-ad5f-1f8e7b6448f1; April Gordon, "A New Eurasian Far Right Rising: Reflections on Ukraine, Georgia, and Armenia," Freedom House Special Report, January 2020, https:// freedomhouse.org/report/special-report/2020/new-eurasian-far -right-rising; William A. Galston, "The Rise of European Populism and the Collapse of the Center-Left," Brookings Institution, March 8, 2018, https://www.brookings.edu/blog/order-from-chaos/2018/03/08/the -rise-of-european-populism-and-the-collapse-of-the-center-left.

26 **trend in the world:** Freedom House, "Freedom in the World 2022."

27 **motivated by special interests:** Mancur Olson, *The Rise and Decline of Nations: Economic Growth, Stagflation, and Social Rigidities* (New Haven: Yale University Press, 1982).

28 **most Americans support gun control measures:** "Amid a Series of

Mass Shootings in the U.S., Gun Policy Remains Deeply Divisive," Pew Research Center, April 20, 2021, https://www.pewresearch.org/politics /2021/04/20/amid-a-series-of-mass-shootings-in-the-u-s-gun-policy-remains-deeply-divisive.

28 **woman's right to choose:** Hannah Hartig, "About Six-in-Ten Americans Say Abortion Should Be Legal in All or Most Cases," Pew Research Center, June 13, 2022, https://www.pewresearch.org/fact-tank/2022 /06/13/about-six-in-ten-americans-say-abortion-should-be-legal-in -all-or-most-cases-2.

28 **inequality is large and growing:** Congressional Budget Office, "The Distribution of Household Income, 2018" (Washington, D.C.: Congressional Budget Office, 2021), 36–38, https://www.cbo.gov/system/files/2021 -08/57061-Distribution-Household-Income.pdf.

29 **"inequality destroys the sense":** George Packer, *Last Best Hope: America in Crisis and Renewal* (New York: Farrar, Straus and Giroux, 2021), 187, 138; In addition, see Evan Osnos, *Wildland: The Making of America's Fury* (New York: Farrar, Straus and Giroux, 2021).

29 **Middle-class incomes remained stagnant:** Drew DeSilver, "For Most U.S. Workers, Real Wages Have Barely Budged in Decades," Pew Research Center, August 7, 2018, https://www.pewresearch.org/fact-tank/2018 /08/07/for-most-us-workers-real-wages-have-barely-budged-for -decades.

29 **Factories closed and jobs disappeared:** Andrew Van Dam, "Millions of Jobs Are Still Missing. Don't Blame Immigrants or Food Stamps," *Washington Post*, February 22, 2018, https://www.washingtonpost.com /news/wonk/wp/2018/02/22/fewer-americans-are-working-dont-blame -immigrants-or-food-stamps; Edward Alden and Laura Taylor-Kale, *The Work Ahead: Machines, Skills, and U.S. Leadership in the Twenty-First Century* (New York: Council on Foreign Relations, 2018).

30 **uncomfortable with cultural and demographic trends:** Brian Resnick, "White Fear of Demographic Change Is a Powerful Psychological Force," *Vox*, last updated January 28, 2017, https://www.vox.com/science -and-health/2017/1/26/14340542/white-fear-trump-psychology -minority-majority. Pew conducted a survey in 2019 and found that

"when asked about the consequences of an increasingly diverse America, nearly half of whites (46%) . . . say a majority-minority country would weaken American customs and values." Kim Parker, Rich Morin, and Juliana Menasce Horowitz, "Looking to the Future, Public Sees an America in Decline on Many Fronts," Pew Research Center, March 21, 2019, https://www.pewresearch.org/social-trends/2019/03/21/public-sees-an-america-in-decline-on-many-fronts.

30 **Americans increasingly feel disillusioned:** "Americans' Views of Government: Low Trust, but Some Positive Performance Ratings," Pew Research Center, September 14, 2020, https://www.pewresearch.org/politics/2020/09/14/americans-views-of-government-low-trust-but-some-positive-performance-ratings; Reid J. Epstein, "As Faith Flags in U.S. Government, Many Voters Want to Upend the System," *New York Times*, July 13, 2022, https://www.nytimes.com/2022/07/13/us/politics/government-trust-voting-poll.html.

30 **57 percent of young people:** Harvard Kennedy School Institute of Politics, "Harvard Youth Poll" (Fall 2021), https://iop.harvard.edu/youth-poll/fall-2021-harvard-youth-poll.

30 **described as wars of choice:** Richard N. Haass, *War of Necessity, War of Choice: A Memoir of Two Iraq Wars* (New York: Simon & Schuster, 2009).

30 **list the Vietnam War:** For more on Vietnam, the best single volume history is Stanley Karnow, *Vietnam: A History*, 2nd ed. (New York: Penguin Books, 1997).

31 **political scientists term "intermediary institutions":** Jan-Werner Müller, *Democracy Rules* (New York: Farrar, Straus and Giroux, 2021).

31 **majority of Americans favor:** "Amid a Series of Mass Shootings in the U.S., Gun Policy Remains Deeply Divisive," Pew Research Center.

31 **even though a majority:** One recent poll found that 63 percent of Americans have positive views on trade. Mohamed Younis, "Sharply Fewer in U.S. View Foreign Trade as Opportunity," Gallup, March 31, 2021, https://news.gallup.com/poll/342419/sharply-fewer-view-foreign-trade-opportunity.aspx.

32 **tends to undermine:** Jonathan Haidt, "Why the Past 10 Years of American Life Have Been Uniquely Stupid," *Atlantic*, April 11, 2022, https://www

.theatlantic.com/magazine/archive/2022/05/social-media-democracy
-trust-babel/629369.

33 **as is increasingly the case:** Ronald F. Inglehart, *Religion's Sudden Decline: What's Causing it, and What Comes Next?* (New York: Oxford University Press, 2021).

33 **"We Americans no longer":** J. Michael Luttig, "Read: J. Michael Luttig's Opening Statement at Jan. 6 Select Committee Hearing," *Politico*, June 16, 2022, https://www.politico.com/news/2022/06/16/j-michael-luttig -opening-statement-jan-6-hearing-00040255.

33 **clustering or sorting:** Robert Putnam observed this phenomenon earlier than most and wrote about the harmful effects this increasing disconnection had on America's civic health. See Robert D. Putnam, *Bowling Alone: The Collapse and Revival of American Community*, rev. ed. (New York: Simon & Schuster, 2000); for more, see Bill Bishop, *The Big Sort: Why the Clustering of Like-Minded America Is Tearing Us Apart* (Boston: Houghton Mifflin Harcourt, 2008).

33 **not widely understood:** Ronald J. Daniels with Grant Shreve and Phillip Spector, *What Universities Owe Democracy* (Baltimore: Johns Hopkins University Press, 2021); for a shorter piece on this theme by the same author, see Ronald J. Daniels, "Universities Are Shunning Their Responsibility to Democracy," *Atlantic*, October 3, 2021, https://www.theatlantic .com/ideas/archive/2021/10/universities-cant-dodge-civics/620261.

33 **what to do to fix things:** For instance, a recent issue of *Democracy: A Journal of Ideas* contains a thought-provoking symposium proposing "the democracy constitution." *Democracy: A Journal of Ideas* 61 (Summer 2021); see also American Academy of Arts and Sciences, *Our Common Purpose: Reinventing American Democracy for the 21st Century* (Cambridge: American Academy of Arts and Sciences, 2020), https://www .amacad.org/sites/default/files/publication/downloads/2020-Democratic -Citizenship_Our-Common-Purpose_0.pdf; E. J. Dionne Jr. and Miles Rapoport, *100% Democracy: The Case for Universal Voting* (New York: The New Press, 2022); J. Michael Luttig, "The Conservative Case for Avoiding a Repeat of Jan. 6," *New York Times*, February 14, 2022, https://www .nytimes.com/2022/02/14/opinion/electoral-count-act.html; Richard

L. Hasen, "Identifying and Minimizing the Risk of Election Subversion and Stolen Elections in the Contemporary United States," *Harvard Law Review*, April 20, 2022, https://harvardlawreview.org/2022/04/identifying -and-minimizing-the-risk-of-election-subversion-and-stolen-elections -in-the-contemporary-united-states; Katherine M. Gehl and Michael E. Porter, "Why Competition in the Politics Industry Is Failing America: A Strategy for Reinvigorating Our Democracy," Harvard Business School, September 2017.

35 **improve the economic situation:** For instance, see Abhijit Banerjee and Esther Duflo, *Good Economics for Hard Times: Better Answers to our Biggest Problems* (New York: PublicAffairs, 2019); Arthur C. Brooks, *The Road to Freedom: How to Win the Fight for Free Enterprise* (New York: Basic Books, 2012); Glenn Hubbard, *The Wall and the Bridge: Fear and Opportunity in Disruption's Wake* (New Haven: Yale University Press, 2022); Annie Lowrey, *Give People Money: How a Universal Basic Income Would End Poverty, Revolutionize Work, and Remake the World* (New York: Crown, 2018); Steven Pearlstein, *Can American Capitalism Survive?: Why Greed Is Not Good, Opportunity Is Not Equal, and Fairness Won't Make Us Poor* (New York: St. Martin's Press, 2018); Robert B. Reich, *Saving Capitalism: For the Many, Not the Few* (New York: Knopf, 2015); and Minouche Shafik, *What We Owe Each Other: A New Social Contract for a Better Society* (Princeton: Princeton University Press, 2021).

PART TWO: THE BILL OF OBLIGATIONS

Obligation I: Be Informed

41 **"wherever the people":** Thomas Jefferson, "Letter from Thomas Jefferson to Richard Price," Library of Congress, January 8, 1789, https://www .loc.gov/exhibits/jefferson/60.html.

41 **"This democracy doesn't work":** Barack Obama, "Barack Obama on His Book, President Trump, George Floyd, the Divisions in the Country, and More," Interview by Scott Pelley, *60 Minutes*, CBS News, November 16,

2020, https://www.cbsnews.com/news/barack-obama-60-minutes
-interview-trump.

42 **"a government which derives":** James Madison, *Federalist*, No. 39, January 16, 1788, Founders Online, National Archives, https://founders
.archives.gov/documents/Madison/01-10-02-0234.

45 **seek to reinforce:** Benjamin R. Barber, *Strong Democracy: Participatory Politics for a New Age* (Berkeley: University of California Press, 2004); Sendhil Mullainathan, "Biased Algorithms Are Easier to Fix Than Biased People," *New York Times*, December 6, 2019, https://www
.nytimes.com/2019/12/06/business/algorithm-bias-fix.html; Farhad Manjoo, "Facebook's Bias Is Built-In, and Bears Watching," *New York Times*, May 11, 2016, https://www.nytimes.com/2016/05/12/technology
/facebooks-bias-is-built-in-and-bears-watching.html.

45 **not research to visit:** Daniel W. Drezner, "How Not to Do Outside Research," *Washington Post*, November 8, 2021, https://www.washington
post.com/outlook/2021/11/08/how-not-do-outside-research.

46 **national debt of the United States:** Alan Rappeport and Jim Tankersley, "U.S. National Debt Tops $31 Trillion for First Time," *New York Times*, October 4, 2022, https://www.nytimes.com/2022/10/04/business
/national-debt.html.

46 **increased 1.1 degrees centigrade:** Rebecca Lindsey and Luann Dahlman, "Climate Change: Global Temperature," Climate.gov, updated June 28, 2022, https://www.climate.gov/news-features/understanding
-climate/climate-change-global-temperature; "World of Change: Global Temperatures," NASA Earth Observatory, accessed April 26, 2022, https://
earthobservatory.nasa.gov/world-of-change/global-temperatures.

47 **stems overwhelmingly from human activity:** Intergovernmental Panel on Climate Change (IPCC), "Climate Change 2021: The Physical Science Basis," *Contribution of Working Group I to the Sixth Assessment Report of the Intergovernmental Panel on Climate Change*, August 7, 2021, https://
www.ipcc.ch/report/ar6/wg1/downloads/report/IPCC_AR6_WGI_SPM
_final.pdf

47 **died of complications:** A recent study that looked at excess mortality

due to the pandemic estimated that the actual number is over 18 million, while another study conducted by the World Health Organization put the death toll at 15 million. "COVID Data Tracker," Centers for Disease Control and Prevention, https://covid.cdc.gov/covid-data-tracker/#datatracker -home; WHO Coronavirus (COVID-19) Dashboard," World Health Organization, https://covid19.who.int/; Haidong Wang et al., "Estimating Excess Mortality Due to the COVID-19 Pandemic: A Systematic Analysis of COVID-19-related Mortality, 2020–21," *Lancet* 399, no. 10334 (March 10, 2022):1513–36; World Health Organization, "14.9 Million Excess Deaths Associated with the COVID-19 Pandemic in 2020 and 2021," May 5, 2022, https://www.who.int/news/item/05-05-2022-14.9-million-excess-deaths -were-associated-with-the-COVID-19-pandemic-in-2020-and-2021.

48 **"everyone is entitled":** Daniel Patrick Moynihan, "More Than Social Security Was at Stake," *Washington Post*, January 18, 1983.

48 **"COVID vaccines are safe":** Katie Robertson, "The Associated Press Names a New Top Editor," *New York Times*, September 1, 2021, https:// www.nytimes.com/2021/09/01/business/media/associated-press-new -editor.html.

48 **"Truth is non-negotiable":** Matthew Garrahan, "Fox News Anchor Chris Wallace: 'There's No Spin to Truth,'" *Financial Times*, November 12, 2021, https://www.ft.com/content/6e52ff30-cc94-4e27-a922-0021c3156270.

48 **administered to billions:** Lisa Maragakis and Gabor David Kelen, "Is the COVID-19 Vaccine Safe?," Johns Hopkins Medicine, last updated January 4, 2022, https://www.hopkinsmedicine.org/health/conditions -and-diseases/coronavirus/is-the-covid19-vaccine-safe; Anne Hause, James Baggs, and Paige Marquez, et al., "Safety Monitoring of COVID-19 Vaccine Booster Doses Among Persons Aged 12–17 Years—United States, December 9, 2021–February 20, 2022," *Morbidity and Mortality Weekly Report* 71, no. 9 (March 4, 2022): 347–51.

48 **two degrees Fahrenheit:** IPCC, "Climate Change 2021: The Physical Science Basis."

48 **results show that nothing occurred:** Cassidy, "Far Too Little Vote Fraud."

49 **August 2021 UN report:** IPCC, "Climate Change 2021: The Physical Science Basis."

49 **Iraq had weapons of mass destruction:** Richard Haass, *War of Necessity, War of Choice: A Memoir of Two Iraq Wars*; "Full Text of U.S. Secretary of State Colin Powell's Speech to the United Nations on Iraq," *Washington Post*, February 5, 2003, https://www.washingtonpost.com /wp-srv/nation/transcripts/powelltext_020503.html.

Obligation II: Get Involved

53 **"Governments are instituted":** *Declaration of Independence.*

54 **one-third to 40 percent:** Jordan Misra, "Voter Turnout Rates Among All Voting Age and Major Racial and Ethnic Groups Were Higher Than in 2014," United States Census Bureau, April 23, 2019, https://www.census .gov/library/stories/2019/04/behind-2018-united-states-midterm -election-turnout.html; Kevin Schaul, Kate Rabinowitz, and Ted Mellnik, "2020 Turnout Is the Highest in over a Century," *Washington Post*, November 5, 2020, https://www.washingtonpost.com/graphics/2020 /elections/voter-turnout.

54 **survey of thirty-five democracies:** Drew DeSilver, "In Past Elections, U.S. Trailed Most Developed Countries in Voter Turnout," Pew Research Center, November 3, 2020, https://www.pewresearch.org/fact-tank/2020 /11/03/in-past-elections-u-s-trailed-most-developed-countries-in-voter -turnout.

54 **reasons people give:** Mallory Newall and Sara Machi, "Why Don't People Vote?," Ipsos, December 15, 2020, https://www.ipsos.com/en-us/news -polls/medill-npr-nonvoters-2020; Katie Livingstone, "November 2020: Counted Out," Medill School of Journalism, December 15, 2020, https:// dc.medill.northwestern.edu/blog/2020/12/15/nonvoters-2020-counted -out/#sthash.mnie1wm0.dpbs.

56 **activists passed an amendment:** Dan Barry, "One Small Step for Democracy in a 'Live Free or Die' Town," *New York Times*, July 10, 2022, https:// www.nytimes.com/2022/07/10/us/croydon-free-state-politics.html.

57 **"The impact of participation":** James Mattis, "The Enemy Within," *Atlantic*, December 2019, https://www.theatlantic.com/magazine/archive /2019/12/james-mattis-the-enemy-within/600781.

57 **successful recall of three:** Thomas Fuller, "In Landslide, San Francisco Forces Out 3 Board of Education Members," *New York Times*, February 16, 2022, https://www.nytimes.com/2022/02/16/us/san-francisco-school -board-recall.html.

57 **Mothers Against Drunk Driving (MADD):** Frank J. Weed, "The MADD Queen: Charisma and the Founder of Mothers Against Drunk Driving," *The Leadership Quarterly* 4, no. 3–4 (1993), 329–46.

58 **used social media to launch:** Sam Levine, "Republicans Tried to Rig the Vote in Michigan—but 'Political Novices' Just Defeated Them," *Guardian*, November 27, 2019, https://www.theguardian.com/us-news/2019/nov /27/gerrymandering-michigan-citizens-voters-not-politicians; Katie Fahey, "My Fight Against Gerrymandering," *New York Times*, January 23, 2018, https://www.nytimes.com/video/opinion/100000005675457/my -fight-against-gerrymandering.html.

58 **parents at school board meetings:** Margaret Talbot, "The Increasingly Wild World of School-Board Meetings," *New Yorker*, October 8, 2021, https://www.newyorker.com/news/daily-comment/the-increasingly -wild-world-of-school-board-meetings.

58 **"All great change in America":** Ronald Reagan, "Farewell Address to the Nation" (speech, Washington, D.C., January 11, 1989), Ronald Reagan Presidential Library and Museum, National Archives, https://www.rea ganlibrary.gov/archives/speech/farewell-address-nation.

Obligation III: Stay Open to Compromise

63 **"I reject the word":** John Boehner, "Meet the Next House Speaker, Rep. John Boehner," interview by Lesley Stahl, *60 Minutes*, CBS News, https://www.cbsnews.com/news/meet-the-next-house-speaker-rep-john -boehner.

63 **"Compromise need not":** John F. Kennedy, *Profiles in Courage* (New York: Harper & Brothers, 1956), 40.

64 **"the compacts which are to embrace":** Alexander Hamilton, *Federalist*, No. 85, *Federalist Papers: Primary Documents in American History*, Library of Congress, https://guides.loc.gov/federalist-papers/text-81-85.

64 **compromises, including that of 1790:** Ron Chernow, *Alexander Hamilton* (New York: Penguin Press, 2004).

65 **"All legislation, all government, all society":** Mitch McConnell and Roy E. Brownell II, *The U.S. Senate and the Commonwealth: Kentucky Lawmakers and the Evolution of Legislative Leadership* (Lexington, Kentucky: University Press of Kentucky, 2019).

65 **"If you got 75":** Reagan, *An American Life* (New York: Simon & Schuster, 1990), 171.

68 **came together to reflect:** For more on how this compromise was reached, see Annie Karni and Emily Cochrane, "Leaving Wish Lists at the Door, Senators Found Consensus on Guns," *New York Times,* June 24, 2022, https://www.nytimes.com/2022/06/24/us/politics/guns-bill-senate-negotiations.html; for public polling on support for additional gun laws, see "Broad Public Approval of New Gun Law, but Few Say It Will Do a Lot To Stem Gun Violence," Pew Research Center, July 11, 2022, https://www.pewresearch.org/politics/2022/07/11/broad-public-approval-of-new-gun-law-but-few-say-it-will-do-a-lot-to-stem-gun-violence.

69 **best alternative to a negotiated agreement:** Roger Fisher and William Ury, *Getting to Yes: Negotiating Agreement Without Giving In,* 3rd ed. (New York: Penguin Books, 2011).

70 **Cuban Missile Crisis:** Graham T. Allison and Philip D. Zelikow, *Essence of Decision: Explaining the Cuban Missile Crisis* (Harlow/Essex, UK: Longman, 1999).

71 **"Read my lips":** George H. W. Bush, "Address Accepting the Presidential Nomination at the Republican National Convention in New Orleans" (speech, New Orleans, LA, August 18, 1988), The American Presidency Project, https://www.presidency.ucsb.edu/documents/address-accepting-the-presidential-nomination-the-republican-national-convention-new.

Obligation IV: Remain Civil

75 **"civility is not a sign":** John F. Kennedy, "Inaugural Address" (speech, Washington, D.C., January 20, 1961), The American Presidency Project, https://www.presidency.ucsb.edu/documents/inaugural-address-2.

75 **"Civility is not a tactic":** George W. Bush, "First Inaugural Address" (speech, Washington, D.C., January 20, 2001), The American Presidency Project, https://www.presidency.ucsb.edu/documents/inaugural -address-52.

76 **Why is this concept so important?:** For a thoughtful discussion on civility, see Stephen L. Carter, *Civility: Manners, Morals, and the Etiquette of Democracy* (New York: Basic Books, 1998).

78 **"When the facts change":** There is some debate on whether Keynes ever actually uttered this phrase. For instance, see Jason Zweig, "Keynes: He Didn't Say Half of What He Said. Or Did He?," *Wall Street Journal*, February 11, 2011, https://www.wsj.com/articles/BL-MB-32547.

80 **lack of civility also derives:** According to one survey, one in five Americans say they seldom or never interact with someone who does not share their race or ethnicity or religion, while nearly one quarter say they seldom or never interact with someone from a different political party. Maxine Najle and Robert P. Jones, "American Democracy in Crisis: The Fate of Pluralism in a Divided Nation," PRRI, February 19, 2019, https://www.prri.org/research/american-democracy-in-crisis-the -fate-of-pluralism-in-a-divided-nation. Another survey found that half of "consistent conservatives" and 35 percent of "consistent liberals" say it is important to them to live in a place where most people share their political views. "Section 3: Political Polarization and Personal Life," Pew Research Center, June 12, 2014, https://www.pewresearch.org/politics /2014/06/12/section-3-political-polarization-and-personal-life.

80 **reinforces divisions and intolerance:** Bill Bishop, *The Big Sort: Why the Clustering of Like-Minded America Is Tearing Us Apart* (Boston: Houghton Mifflin Harcourt, 2008).

81 **tales of the friendship between:** Jennifer Senior, "The Ginsburg-Scalia Act Was Not a Farce," *New York Times*, September 22, 2020, https://www .nytimes.com/2020/09/22/opinion/ruth-bader-ginsburg-antonin-scalia .html.

81 **Scalia's dissents forced her:** Following Justice Scalia's passing in 2016, Justice Ginsburg wrote, "We disagreed now and then, but when I wrote for the Court and received a Scalia dissent, the opinion ultimately re-

leased was notably better than my initial circulation." Brett LoGiurato, "Ruth Bader Ginsburg Released a Moving Tribute to Her 'Best Buddy,' Antonin Scalia," *Business Insider*, February 14, 2016, https://www.busi nessinsider.com/ruth-bader-ginsburg-scalia-death-2016-2.

81 **"I attack ideas":** Antonin Scalia, "Justice Scalia on the Record," interview by Lesley Stahl, *60 Minutes*, CBS News, April 24, 2008, https://www .cbsnews.com/news/justice-scalia-on-the-record.

81 **spending some time:** Elizabeth Lesser, "Take 'the Other' to Lunch" (speech, Washington, D.C., December 7, 2010), TED, https://www.ted .com/talks/elizabeth_lesser_take_the_other_to_lunch.

82 **special responsibility to provide forums:** The Dean of Yale's Law School articulated these responsibilities in a letter she wrote to the school's community. Heather K. Gerken, "A Message From Dean Gerken on the March 10 Protest," March 28, 2022, https://law.yale.edu/yls-today /news/message-dean-gerken-march-10-protest.

Obligation V: Reject Violence

87 **has another name: terrorism:** For those interested in learning more about terrorism, the standard work on this subject is Bruce Hoffman, *Inside Terrorism* (New York: Columbia University Press, 2017).

90 **"civil disobedience" can be traced back:** Henry David Thoreau, *Resistance to Civil Government* (1849).

91 **"good trouble, necessary trouble":** Carla D. Hayden, Remembering John Lewis: The Power of 'Good Trouble,'" Library of Congress, July 19, 2020, https://blogs.loc.gov/loc/2020/07/remembering-john-lewis-the -power-of-good-trouble/.

93 **Republican National Committee put forward:** Jonathan Weisman and Reid J. Epstein, "G.O.P. Declares Jan. 6 Attack 'Legitimate Political Discourse.'"

93 **"It was a violent insurrection":** Jonathan Weisman and Annie Karni, "McConnell Denounces R.N.C. Censure of Jan. 6 Panel Members," *New York Times*, February 8, 2022, https://www.nytimes.com/2022/02/08/us /politics/republicans-censure-mcconnell.html.

94 **Supreme Court has ruled:** *Brandenburg v. Ohio*, 395 U.S. 444 (1969).

94 **"likely to incite":** *Brandenburg v. Ohio*, 447.

Obligation VI: Value Norms

97 **Norms are the unwritten traditions:** For an excellent examination of the importance of norms in democracies, see Julia R. Azari and Jennifer K. Smith, "Unwritten Rules: Informal Institutions in Established Democracies," *Perspectives on Politics* 10, no. 1 (March 2012): 37–55.

99 **"Norms are unspoken":** Moisés Naím, "The Dictator's New Playbook," *Foreign Affairs*, March/April 2022, https://www.foreignaffairs.com/articles/world/2022-02-22/dictators-new-playbook.

99 **scale that affects outcomes:** Christina A. Cassidy, "Far Too Little Vote Fraud to Tip Election to Trump, AP Finds," AP News, December 14, 2021, https://apnews.com/article/voter-fraud-election-2020-joe-biden-donald-trump-7fcb6f134e528fee8237c7601db3328f.

100 **"for the sake of our unity":** Al Gore, "Concession Speech" (speech, Washington, D.C., December 13, 2000), *New York Times*, https://www.nytimes.com/2000/12/13/politics/text-of-goreacutes-concession-speech.html.

100 **"it'd tear the country":** Peggy Noonan, "Nixon's Example of Sanity in Washington," *Wall Street Journal*, March 31, 2022, https://www.wsj.com/articles/nixons-example-of-sanity-in-washington-seriousness-maturity-discipline-supreme-court-civil-war-activism-11648764052.

101 **Trump and many of his supporters:** Doug Bock Clark, Alexandra Berzon, and Kirsten Berg, "Building the 'Big Lie': Inside the Creation of Trump's Stolen Election Myth," ProPublica, April 26, 2022, https://www.propublica.org/article/big-lie-trump-stolen-election-inside-creation.

101 **done by the leading:** Nick Corasaniti, "False Election Claims in California Reveal a New Normal for G.O.P.," *New York Times*, last updated October 11, 2021, https://www.nytimes.com/2021/09/12/us/politics/gop-voter-fraud-california-recall.html.

101 **"the enemy of the people":** Emily Stewart, "Trump Calls Media the 'True Enemy of the People' the Same Day a Bomb Is Sent to CNN," *Vox*,

October 29, 2018, https://www.vox.com/policy-and-politics/2018/10
/29/18037894/donald-trump-twitter-media-enemy-pittsburgh.

101 **flawed decision-making:** As Supreme Court Justice Hugo Black wrote,
"Only a free and unrestrained press can effectively expose deception in
government. And paramount among the responsibilities of a free press
is the duty to prevent any part of the government from deceiving the
people and sending them off to distant lands to die of foreign fevers and
foreign shot and shell. In my view, far from deserving condemnation for
their courageous reporting, the *New York Times*, the *Washington Post*,
and other newspapers should be commended for serving the purpose
that the Founding Fathers saw so clearly. In revealing the workings of
government that led to the Vietnam war, the newspapers nobly did precisely that which the Founders hoped and trusted they would do." *New
York Times Co. v. United States*, 403 U.S. 713 (1971), 717.

101 **"Were it left to me":** Thomas Jefferson, "From Thomas Jefferson to Edward Carrington, 16 January 1787," Founders Online, National Archives,
https://founders.archives.gov/documents/Jefferson/01-11-02-0047.

102 **Recusing or removing oneself:** Notably, Supreme Court Justice Clar-
ence Thomas has not recused himself from cases concerning efforts
to overturn the 2020 presidential election, even though his wife was
deeply involved in efforts to do so. Adam Liptak, "Justice Thomas Ruled
on Election Cases. Should His Wife's Texts Have Stopped Him?," *New
York Times*, March 25, 2022, https://www.nytimes.com/2022/03/25/us
/supreme-court-clarence-thomas-recusal.html; Jane Mayer, "Legal
Scholars Are Shocked By Ginni Thomas's 'Stop the Steal' Texts," *New
Yorker*, March 25, 2022, https://www.newyorker.com/news/news-desk
/legal-scholars-are-shocked-by-ginni-thomass-stop-the-steal-texts.

104 **Hatch Act bans:** 5 U.S.C. §§ 7321–7326, available at https://osc.gov
/Services/Pages/HatchAct.aspx.

105 **not all can be counted on:** For instance, several U.S. senators were
found to have sold off their personal stocks in the early days of the
COVID-19 pandemic after receiving briefings about the potential seri-
ousness of the pandemic. Ella Nilsen, "Senators Allegedly Dumping Stock
as the Market Tanks Is Why Some People Think Senators Shouldn't Own

Stock," *Vox*, March 20, 2020, https://www.vox.com/2020/3/20/21188144 /senators-dumping-stock-as-market-tanks. Congressman Chris Collins resigned his seat before pleading guilty to insider trading in 2020. Benjamin Weiser and Emily Palmer, "Ex-Rep. Chris Collins Gets 26-Month Prison Sentence in Insider Trading Case," *New York Times*, last updated June 24 2020, https://www.nytimes.com/2020/01/17/nyregion/chris -collins-sentencing-prison.html. Following these revelations, U.S. Senators Jon Ossoff (D-GA) and Mark Kelly (D-AZ) have introduced legislation to ban all members of Congress as well as their spouses and dependents from trading stocks. While House Speaker Nancy Pelosi was initially opposed to such a law, in early 2022 congressional leadership became more receptive to the idea, which has the support of most Americans.

Obligation VII: Promote the Common Good

109 **"No man is an island"**: John Donne, "Meditation XVII," *Devotions upon Emergent Occasions.*

109 **"Look not every man"**: Philippians 2:4 (King James Version), available at https://quod.lib.umich.edu/cgi/k/kjv/kjv-idx?type=DIV1&byte=5200653.

109 **"all of Israel"**: This phrase comes from the Talmud (Shevuot 39a), which states "*kol yisrael arevim zeh bazeh*" and forms the basis of the concept of communal responsibility in Jewish law. This portion of the Talmud can be found at https://www.sefaria.org/Shevuot.39a.22 ?ven=William_Davidson_Edition_-_English&vhe=Wikisource_Talmud _Bavli&lang=bi.

110 **world as one family:** For instance, look to Bhagavad Gita 5:18 and 6:9 or the phrase "*vasudhaiva kutumbakam*" (the world is one family), taken from the Maha Upanishad 6:72.

110 **"We are caught in"**: Martin Luther King Jr., "Letter from a Birmingham Jail," April 16, 1963, available at http://okra.stanford.edu/transcription /document_images/undecided/630416-019.pdf.

110 **"our relations with"**: Theodore Roosevelt, "Inaugural Address" (speech, Washington, D.C., March 4, 1905), The American Presidency Project, https://www.presidency.ucsb.edu/documents/inaugural-address-45.

111 **Harm Principle, which argues:** John Stuart Mill, *On Liberty* (1859).

111 **"your right to swing":** Zechariah Chafee Jr., "Freedom of Speech in War Time," *Harvard Law Review* 32, no. 8 (June 1919): 957.

113 **save some fifteen thousand lives:** National Highway Traffic Safety Administration, "Seat Belts Save Lives," United States Department of Transportation, accessed April 27, 2022, https://www.nhtsa.gov/seat-belts /seat-belts-save-lives.

113 **Many Americans reject:** According to a recent survey, one-quarter of Americans are opposed to requiring that masks be worn on public transportation. "Support for Mask Requirements in Public Persists Although Worries about Infection Continue to Decline," AP-NORC Center for Public Affairs Research, April 2022, https://apnorc.org/projects /support-for-mask-requirements-in-public-persists-although-worries -about-infection-continue-to-decline. Another recent poll found that 56 percent of U.S. adults said they backed COVID-19 vaccination requirements from employers, while one-third opposed such a requirement. Gaby Galvin, "Following Supreme Court's Decision to Nix Federal Vaccine Requirement for Private Workers, More Than 1 in 2 Adults Say They Back Mandates by Employers," Morning Consult, January 19, 2022, https://morningconsult.com/2022/01/19/employer-COVID-vaccine -mandate-supreme-court-poll. This is yet another issue where there is a stark political divide; only 19 percent of Republicans polled supported a vaccine requirement for federal government workers, while 94 percent of Democrats supported such a requirement. Jeffrey M. Jones, "Majority in U.S. Supports Biden COVID-19 Vaccine Mandates," Gallup, September 24, 2021, https://news.gallup.com/poll/354983 /majority-supports-biden-COVID-vaccine-mandates.aspx; Emma G. Fitzsimmons, "N.Y.C. fires 1,430 workers, less than 1 percent of city employees, over a vaccine mandate," *New York Times*, February 14, 2022, https://www.nytimes.com/2022/02/14/nyregion/nyc-vaccine -mandate.html.

114 **"the liberty secured":** *Jacobson v. Massachusetts*, 197 U.S. 11 (1905), 11.

114 **"There is, of course, a sphere":** *Jacobson v. Massachusetts*, 197 U.S. 11 (1905), 29.

115 **effectiveness, its pristine safety record:** Lisa Maragakis and Gabor David Kelen, "Is the COVID-19 Vaccine Safe?," Johns Hopkins Medicine, last updated January 4, 2022, https://www.hopkinsmedicine.org/health /conditions-and-diseases/coronavirus/is-the-covid19-vaccine-safe; Anne Hause, James Baggs, and Paige Marquez et al., "Safety Monitoring of COVID-19 Vaccine Booster Doses Among Persons Aged 12–17 Years," *Morbidity and Mortality Weekly Report* 71, no. 9 (March 4, 2022): 347–51.

115 **more than one million:** "COVID Data Tracker," Centers for Disease Control and Prevention; Haidong Wang et al., "Estimating Excess Mortality Due to the COVID-19 Pandemic: A Systematic Analysis of COVID-19-Related Mortality, 2020–21," *Lancet* 399, no. 10334 (March 10, 2022): 1513–36; World Health Organization, "14.9 Million Excess Deaths Associated with the COVID-19 Pandemic in 2020 and 2021," May 5, 2022, https://www.who.int/news/item/05-05-2022-14.9-million-excess-deaths -were-associated-with-the-COVID-19-pandemic-in-2020-and-2021.

117 **Equal opportunity is not to be equated:** Richard V. Reeves, *Saving Horatio Alger: Equality, Opportunity, and the American Dream* (Washington, D.C.: Brookings Institution Press, 2014).

118 **"a great equalizer":** David Rhode, Kristina Cooke, and Himanshu-Ojha, "The Decline of the 'Great Equalizer,'" *Atlantic*, December 19, 2012, https:// www.theatlantic.com/business/archive/2012/12/the-decline-of-the -great-equalizer/266455.

118 **race could be taken into account:** *Grutter v. Bollinger*, 539 U.S. 306 (2003).

119 **legacy or institutional admissions:** Stephanie Saul, "Elite Colleges' Quiet Fight to Favor Alumni Children," *New York Times*, July 13, 2022, https://www.nytimes.com/2022/07/13/us/legacy-admissions-colleges -universities.html.

Obligation VIII: Respect Government Service

124 **"the nine most terrifying words":** Ronald Reagan, "Transcript of President Reagan's News Conference," *Washington Post*, August 13, 1986, https://www.washingtonpost.com/archive/politics/1986/08/13/tran

script-of-president-reagans-news-conference/bceaa7d7-a544-4c4e
-8af1-51f303a00e25.

124 **"Government's view of the economy":** Ronald Reagan, "Remarks to State Chairpersons of the National White House Conference on Small Business" (speech, Washington, D.C., August 15, 1986), Ronald Reagan Presidential Library & Museum, https://www.reaganlibrary.gov/archives /speech/remarks-state-chairpersons-national-white-house-conference -small-business.

124 **polls indicate that public trust:** "Public Trust in Government: 1958–2021," Pew Research Center, May 17, 2021, https://www.pewresearch.org/politics /2021/05/17/public-trust-in-government-1958-2021.

124 **more trusting of government:** "Public Trust in Government: 1958–2021," Pew Research Center.

126 **9 million Americans:** Fiona Hill, "Public Service and the Federal Government," Brookings Institution, May 27, 2020, https://www.brook ings.edu/policy2020/votervital/public-service-and-the-federal -government; "Budget Projections for FY22 (as of May 25, 2022)," Congressional Budget Office, accessed October 21, 2022, https://www.cbo .gov/topics/budget.

126 **four thousand people:** "Political Appointee Tracker," Partnership for Public Service and the *Washington Post*, https://ourpublicservice.org /performance-measures/political-appointee-tracker.

127 **proposal reportedly under consideration:** Jonathan Swan, "A Radical Plan for Trump's Second Term," Axios, July 22, 2022, https://www.axios .com/2022/07/22/trump-2025-radical-plan-second-term.

127 **common experience would help:** Evan Osnos, "Can a Vastly Bigger National-Service Program Bring the Country Back Together?," *New Yorker*, November 19, 2021, https://www.newyorker.com/news/daily -comment/can-a-vastly-bigger-national-service-program-bring-the -country-back-together.

128 **almost half of second-year:** Mark Murray, "A New Political Divide: Nearly Half of College Students Wouldn't Room with Someone Who Votes Differently," NBC News, August 18, 2022, https://www.nbcnews

.com/meet-the-press/first-read/new-political-divide-nearly-half
-college-students-wouldnt-room-someone-rcna43609.

128 **create a "Civilian Climate Corps":** Tik Root, "9 Questions about the
Civilian Climate Corps, Answered," *Washington Post*, September 16, 2021,
https://www.washingtonpost.com/climate-solutions/2021/09/16/civilian
-climate-corps-explained.

129 **"promote national unity":** Decree No. 51 of June 16, 1933, puts forward
the objectives of the National Youth Service Corps (NYSC), which can
be found at https://www.nysc.gov.ng/objectives.html.

129 **Several European countries are debating:** Elisabeth Braw, "Ask What
You Can Do for Your Country," *Foreign Policy*, August 4, 2020, https://
foreignpolicy.com/2020/08/04/national-service-germany-usa-ask-what
-you-can-do-for-your-country.

Obligation IX: Support the Teaching of Civics

134 **this case the American nation:** Jill Lepore, "A New Americanism: Why
a Nation Needs a National Story," *Foreign Affairs*, March/April 2019,
https://www.foreignaffairs.com/articles/united-states/2019-02-05
/new-americanism-nationalism-jill-lepore.

135 **"This national feeling":** Ronald Reagan, "Farewell Address to the Nation"
(speech, Washington, D.C., January 11, 1989), Ronald Reagan Presidential
Library and Museum, National Archives, https://www.reaganlibrary
.gov/archives/speech/farewell-address-nation.

135 **Many schools do not:** Ashley Jeffrey and Scott Sargrad, "Strengthening
Democracy With a Modern Civics Education," Center for American
Progress, December 14, 2019, https://www.americanprogress.org/article
/strengthening-democracy-modern-civics-education; Michael Hansen,
Elizabeth Levesque, Jon Valant, and Diana Quintero, "The 2018 Brown
Center Report on American Education: How Well Are American Students
Learning?," Brookings Institution, June 2018, https://www.brookings.edu
/wp-content/uploads/2018/06/2018-Brown-Center-Report-on-American
-Education_FINAL1.pdf.

137 **our civics deficit:** George Packer, "Can Civics Save America?," *Atlantic*,

May 15, 2021, https://www.theatlantic.com/ideas/archive/2021/05/civics
-education-1619-crt/618894.

137 **eight states and the District of Columbia:** Jeffrey and Sargrad,
"Strengthening Democracy With a Modern Civics Education." In the
time since this report was published, Oregon's legislature adopted a bill
requiring students to earn 0.5 civics course credits to graduate, beginning with the class of 2026. Thus, as of May 2022, thirty-one states require half a year of civics education. This number may rise in the
coming years, as additional states are weighing similar legislation.
Oregon's law can be accessed at https://olis.oregonlegislature.gov/liz
/2021R1/Downloads/MeasureDocument/SB513.

137 **One state (Hawai'i):** Jeffrey and Sargrad, "Strengthening Democracy
With a Modern Civics Education."; "Graduation Requirements," Hawai'i
State Department of Education, accessed April 27, 2022, https://www
.hawaiipublicschools.org/TeachingAndLearning/StudentLearning/
GraduationRequirements/Pages/Requirements.aspx.

137 **is so uneven:** Jeremy A. Stern et al., "State of State Standards for Civics and U.S. History in 2021," Thomas B. Fordham Institute, June 2021,
https://fordhaminstitute.org/national/research/state-state-standards
-civics-and-us-history-2021.

137 **Less than a fifth:** American Council of Trustees and Alumni, *A Crisis
in Civic Education* (Washington, D.C.: American Council of Trustees
and Alumni, 2016), https://www.goacta.org/wp-content/uploads/ee
/download/A_Crisis_in_Civic_Education.pdf.

137 **tend to be worse:** American Council of Trustees and Alumni, *No U.S.
History? How College History Departments Leave the United States Out of
the Major,* 2nd ed. (Washington, D.C.: American Council of Trustees and
Alumni, 2021), https://www.goacta.org/wp-content/uploads/2021/11
/No.-U.S.-History_2.pdf.

137 **they are not required:** American Council of Trustees and Alumni, *A
Crisis in Civic Education.*

138 **know and understand little:** "Americans Are Poorly Informed About
Basic Constitutional Provisions," Annenberg Public Policy Center of the
University of Pennsylvania, September 12, 2017, https://www.annenberg

publicpolicycenter.org/americans-are-poorly-informed-about-basic
-constitutional-provisions. More recent polls show some signs of progress, but knowledge of civics is still not anywhere close to where it
needs to be. "Amid Pandemic and Protests, Civics Survey Finds Americans Know More of Their Rights," Annenberg Public Policy Center of the
University of Pennsylvania, September 14, 2020, https://www.annen
bergpublicpolicycenter.org/pandemic-protests-2020-civics-survey
-americans-know-much-more-about-their-rights.

138 **do not value it highly:** One poll found that only 45 percent of Americans surveyed are satisfied with the way democracy is working. Richard
Wike, Laura Silver, Shannon Schumacher, and Aidan Connaughton,
"Many in U.S., Western Europe Say Their Political System Needs Major
Reform," Pew Research Center, March 31, 2021, https://www.pew
research.org/global/2021/03/31/many-in-us-western-europe-say
-their-political-system-needs-major-reform.

138 **One-third believe violent action:** Dan Balz, Scott Clement, and Emily
Guskin, "Republicans and Democrats Divided over Jan. 6 Insurrection
and Trump's Culpability, Post-UMD Poll Finds," *Washington Post*, January 1, 2022, https://www.washingtonpost.com/politics/2022/01/01/post
-poll-january-6.

138 **thirteen thousand districts:** Maya Riser-Kositsky, "Education Statistics: Facts About American Schools," *Education Week*, last updated
August 2, 2022, https://www.edweek.org/leadership/education-statistics
-facts-about-american-schools/2019/01.

139 **60 percent of high school graduates:** U.S. Department of Education,
National Center for Education Statistics, *The Condition of Education
2021* (2021-144), https://nces.ed.gov/programs/coe/indicator/cpa.

139 **have a core curriculum:** Columbia College is notable in this regard.

139 **"Our curricula have abdicated":** Ronald J. Daniels, "What Universities
Owe Democracy," *Democracy: A Journal of Ideas*, no. 64 (Spring 2022):
https://democracyjournal.org/magazine/64/what-universities-owe
-democracy.

142 **1619 and 1776 projects:** The 1619 Project is the *New York Times Magazine*'s attempt to reframe American history by putting "slavery and its

continuing legacy at the center of our national narrative." The project can be accessed at https://www.nytimes.com/interactive/2019/08/14 /magazine/1619-america-slavery.html. In response, President Trump launched "The President's Advisory 1776 Commission," which in January 2021 released its own report that can be accessed at https://trumpwhite house.archives.gov/wp-content/uploads/2021/01/The-Presidents -Advisory-1776-Commission-Final-Report.pdf.

142 **debate competing interpretations:** Robert Litan, *Resolved: Debate Can Revolutionize Education and Help Save Our Democracy* (Washington, D.C.: Brookings Institution Press, 2020).

142 **students participate in:** The Council on Foreign Relations, where I currently serve as president, has created free National Security Council and UN Security Council simulations, as well as a "Convene the Council" game that focuses on foreign policy and civics education. These resources can be found at https://modeldiplomacy.cfr.org/ and https:// www.icivics.org/games/convene-council.

143 **"Nothing in this Act":** "Civics Secures Democracy Act," S. 879, 117th Cong, 2021, Sec 2. (b).

Obligation X: Put Country First

147 **"The powers not delegated":** U.S. Const., amend. X.

148 **"We shall nobly save":** Abraham Lincoln, "Annual Message to Congress—Concluding Remarks" (speech, Washington, D.C., December 1, 1862), Abraham Lincoln Online, https://www.abrahamlincolnonline .org/lincoln/speeches/congress.htm.

148 **"To suppose that any form":** James Madison, "Judicial Powers of the National Government" (speech, Richmond, Virginia, June 20, 1788), Founders Online, National Archives, https://founders.archives.gov /documents/Madison/01-11-02-0101.

148 **"The public interest depends":** George W. Bush, "Second Inaugural Address" (speech, Washington, D.C., January 20, 2005), *The American Presidency Project*, https://www.presidency.ucsb.edu/documents/inaugural -address-13.

149 **confirmed in the final year:** Timothy B. Lee, "At Least 14 Supreme Court Justices Have Been Confirmed During Election Years," *Vox*, February 13, 2016, https://www.vox.com/2016/2/13/10987692/14-supreme -court-confirmations.

150 **ruled in June 2022 to overturn:** The majority opinion of *Dobbs v. Jackson Women's Health Organization*, delivered by Justice Samuel Alito, the concurring opinion by Chief Justice John Roberts that focused on the question of judicial restraint, and the powerful dissent by Justices Stephen Breyer, Sonia Sotomayor, and Elena Kagan (that among other things highlighted stare decisis) can all be found at https://www .supremecourt.gov/opinions/21pdf/19-1392_6j37.pdf.

152 **"Some were courageous":** John F. Kennedy, *Profiles in Courage* (New York: Harper & Brothers, 1956), 40.

152 **"I am persuaded":** Kennedy, *Profiles in Courage*, 258.

152 **"His desire to win":** Kennedy, *Profiles in Courage*, 259.

152 **Trump made conditional:** "Full Document: Trump's Call With the Ukrainian President," *New York Times*, October 30, 2019, https://www .nytimes.com/interactive/2019/09/25/us/politics/trump-ukraine -transcript.html.

153 **the conversation as "perfect":** Donald Trump, "Remarks by President Trump and President Niinistö of the Republic of Finland in Joint Press Conference," October 2, 2019, https://trumpwhitehouse.archives.gov /briefings-statements/remarks-president-trump-president-niinisto -republic-finland-joint-press-conference.

Conclusion

155 **"Government is a relation":** Franklin D. Roosevelt, "Commonwealth Club Address" (speech, San Francisco, California, September 23, 1932), Center for American Progress, https://images2.americanprogress.org /campus/email/FDRCommonwealthClubAddress.pdf.

156 **"Rugged individualism is not sufficient":** Harvard University Committee, *General Education in a Free Society: Report of the Committee* (Cambridge: Harvard University Press, 1945), 76–77.

158 **the decision of several Democratic:** Jonathan Weisman, "Democrats' Risky Bet: Aid G.O.P. Extremists in Spring, Hoping to Beat Them in Fall," *New York Times*, June 16, 2022, https://www.nytimes.com/2022 /06/16/us/politics/democrats-midterms-trump-gop.html.

161 **"a bad cause seldom":** James Madison, *Federalist*, No. 41, Library of Congress, https://guides.loc.gov/federalist-papers/text-41-50.

INDEX

INDEX